The Young Adult's Guide to

Selling Your Art, Music, Writing, Photography, & Crafts

ONLINE

Turn Your Hobby into Cash

Ann O'Phelan

THE YOUNG ADULT'S GUIDE TO SELLING YOUR ART, MUSIC, WRITING, PHOTOGRAPHY, & CRAFTS ONLINE: TURN YOUR HOBBY INTO CASH

1405 SW 6th Avenue • Ocala, Florida 34471 • Phone 800-814-1132 • Fax 352-622-1875
Website: www.atlantic-pub.com • Email: sales@atlantic-pub.com
SAN Number: 268-1250

Library of Congress Cataloging-in-Publication Data

Names: O'Phelan, Ann Marie, 1960- author.
Title: The young adult's guide to selling your art, music, writing,
  photography, & crafts online : turn your hobby into cash / by Ann O'Phelan.
Other titles: Young adult's guide to selling your art, music, writing,
  photography, and crafts online
Description: Ocala, Florida : Atlantic Publishing Group, Inc., [2017] |
  Includes bibliographical references and index.
Identifiers: LCCN 2017018374 (print) | LCCN 2017030968 (ebook) | ISBN
  9781620231784 (ebook) | ISBN 9781620231777 (alk. paper) | ISBN 1620231778 (alk.
  paper)
Subjects: LCSH: Selling--Handicraft. | Handicraft--Internet marketing. |
  Electronic commerce.
Classification: LCC HF5439.H27 (ebook) | LCC HF5439.H27 O64 2017 (print) |
  DDC 658.8/777--dc23
LC record available at https://lccn.loc.gov/2017018374

Printed in the United States

PROJECT MANAGER: Lisa McGinnes • lmcginnes@atlantic-pub.com
INTERIOR LAYOUT AND JACKET DESIGN: Nicole Sturk • nicolejonessturk@gmail.com

Reduce. Reuse.
RECYCLE.

A decade ago, Atlantic Publishing signed the Green Press Initiative. These guidelines promote environmentally friendly practices, such as using recycled stock and vegetable-based inks, avoiding waste, choosing energy-efficient resources, and promoting a no-pulping policy. We now use 100-percent recycled stock on all our books. The results: in one year, switching to post-consumer recycled stock saved 24 mature trees, 5,000 gallons of water, the equivalent of the total energy used for one home in a year, and the equivalent of the greenhouse gases from one car driven for a year.

Over the years, we have adopted a number of dogs from rescues and shelters. First there was Bear and after he passed, Ginger and Scout. Now, we have Kira, another rescue. They have brought immense joy and love not just into our lives, but into the lives of all who met them.

We want you to know a portion of the profits of this book will be donated in Bear, Ginger and Scout's memory to local animal shelters, parks, conservation organizations, and other individuals and nonprofit organizations in need of assistance.

– Douglas & Sherri Brown,
President & Vice-President of Atlantic Publishing

Table of Contents

Introduction 13

CHAPTER 1: Why Sell Your Artwork Online? 17

The Benefits of Online Sales Over Traditional Methods..................... 18

The Internet never closes 20

People have different tastes in art 20

A global audience creates more opportunities to reach different types of buyers 20

Selling online minimizes advertising costs 21

Selling online moves your artwork quickly 23

Can You Make Enough Money Selling Art Online? 24

What Art is Being Sold Online? 25

Finding Your Online Niche 25

CHAPTER 2: What You Will Need to Sell Your Products Online.. 29

Your Computer... 29

Hard drive 30

Memory card 31

Processor 32

CD-ROM, CD-RW, DVD-R drive, or flash drive 32

Video card (or graphics card) 33

Sound card.. 33

Computer packages..34

Your Peripherals 35

Video monitor 35

Digital camera 35

Video camera 37

Audio speakers 37

Printer... 38

Scanner 38

Your Internet Service Provider 38

Developing Your Brand...39

Establishing a name and a look 40

Case Study: Kristen Queen 41

Consider colors, fonts, and images.. 42

Finding Out About the Financials...43

Keeping track of inventory, income, expenses, and
business banking 43

Taxes and financial questions 44

CHAPTER 3: Creating a Website 45

Your Domain Name 46

Your Hosting Provider 50

Building Your Website...52

Color 55

Text 56

Image placement 57

Adding Images and Video 57

Images 57

Video 58

Creating Site Maps 58

CHAPTER 4: Search Engines, Maximizing Visitors to
Your Website, and Shipping 61

How results are selected for a search engine query 61

Getting Your Website to Rank High in Search Results 62

Keywords 62

Integrating keywords into your website content 64

Adding readable, useful, keyword optimized content 65

Using keywords in title tags 66

Webpage description 66

Image tags 67

Attracting visitors with faster speeds 67

Completing a test run 68

Cost Considerations 68

CHAPTER 5: Creating a Blog, Enhancing Content, and
Understanding Affiliated Marketing 69

Joining Blogrings 71

Case Study: Zandra Cunningham 72

Providing Informative, Conversational Content 73

    Search for similarities..*74*

    Link building *74*

    Buying links...*74*

Article Writing and Submission 75

    Deciding what to write about *77*

    Submitting your article *78*

Affiliate Marketing 79

CHAPTER 6: Social Media and Discussion Boards...................83

What is Social Marketing? 84

Case Study: Elisa Chong 84

Social Media, Sharing Sites, and Messaging.......................85

    Facebook *85*

    Twitter *86*

    Instagram *87*

    Pinterest *88*

    Snapchat.. *88*

    Flickr *88*

    Instant Messengers *89*

    Bot shops... *89*

    LinkedIn *90*

Discussion Boards 90

    Promoting your works through discussion boards.....................*93*

    Using your profile and personal signature to drive traffic *95*

CHAPTER 7: Selling Your Products Through Etsy, Artfire, Handmade at Amazon, and Spreesy 97

Using Your Art to Create Your Online Identity 98

Etsy.. 99

Case Study: Moziah "Mo" Bridges................................. 100

ArtFire 104

Handmade at Amazon... 106

Spreesy.. 108

CHAPTER 8: Where Else Can You Sell Online? 111

Creative Sites and Classifieds 112

Artwork, images, and photographs............................. 112

Music 114

Audio and video 115

Other places to consider.. 116

What to Watch Out for When Selling Online 117

Keeping track of sales 117

Ensuring your payment 118

Staying safe with online sales connections.................... 118

Reading the reviews 119

Photographing your artwork 120

CHAPTER 9: Participating in Online Auctions.......................... 123

eBay 123

Case Study: Diane Dobson-Barton 124

Setting up your eBay account 126

Listings and fees 127

Building auction listings 129

Choosing the length and timing of your auctions 130

The auction title 130

The auction design 131

The auction text 132

Your "About Me" page 132

Your auction price 133

Case Study: Tanya Bond 134

Your eBay store 134

Artsy 135

CHAPTER 10: Connecting to Your Customers Through Email.. 137

Email 137

Email mini courses 139

Newsletters 141

Never share email addresses with others 143

Update your email list 143

Getting Writing Help 143

Upwork 145

Other Freelance Writer Websites 145

CHAPTER 11: Software and Sites That Offer the
Tools for Success 147

Payment for Your Items 147

Credit card payments made directly on your website 148

PayPal.. 149

Checks and money orders 150

Software and Web Services for Running Your Business 151

Website creation tools... 151

Adobe Dreamweaver CC... 151

PageBreeze.. 152

CGI Form and Autoresponder Tools.. 152

CGI forms... 153

Autoresponders.. 153

Visitor Tracking Software 155

StatCounter 155

OneStatFree... 156

Photo Editing and Video Editing Tools...156

Photo editing 156

Video editing.. 156

Accounting and financial tools...157

Business Plan Tools...158

BPlans 159

Business Plan Pro 160

CHAPTER 12: Where to Turn When You Need Help 161

Need Help Learning the Skills to Set up Your
New Business? 161

On-site classes.. 161

On-site groups 162

Need Help Connecting to Other Artists? 163

 Online groups 163

 On-Site groups 163

Conclusion 165

About the Author 167

Glossary 169

APPENDIX: Shipping Your Works 181

Bibliography 185

Index 187

Introduction

As a creative person, you have probably been told by well-intentioned but misguided friends, family members, career counselors, and teachers that, while creativity is a nice hobby, it is no way to make a living. They may have encouraged you to consider other possibilities, even though those choices might bore the heck out of you.

Many talented artists, crafters, photographers, and musicians spend their days working at jobs they do not like and in environments that do not inspire them or feed their creative natures because they were told that they couldn't make a living as an artist. But you actually can.

Thanks to the Internet, there are now more opportunities than ever for artistic people to realize their dreams. You don't have to live in one of the world's major metropolitan areas to have a chance at artistic success, nor do you have to be represented by a well-known agent. If you have right kind of talent and know how to sell on the Internet, you can do it. It may not be as easy as it sounds, but this book will help you put together a plan of action so you can sell your creative artwork online.

This book is a guide to understanding how to use the Internet to market and sell art, music, photographs, and crafts. It provides specific, step-by-step instructions to create, maintain, and expand a successful online business — and find success doing it.

Within these pages, you will learn:

- How to run your own online business

- How to select the right computer and other hardware

- How to use software programs to help you build your clientele

- How to create a website that showcases your creative works, has a professional look and feel, and makes visitors comfortable with the idea of buying from you

- How to photograph your artwork

- How to accept payments and track orders

- How to use low-cost and free advertising to drive visitors to your website

- How to use online auctions to gain rapid sales

- How to use other websites to promote your artworks, crafts, photographs, and music

- And much more!

This will take hard work and a fair amount of patience to accomplish your success as an online businessperson, but, if you follow the steps, tips, and techniques described in this book, you will have a tremendous advantage that you can use to make art not only your hobby, but also your career.

CHAPTER 1

Why Sell Your Artwork Online?

If you're wondering why you should sell your artwork, crafts, photographs, or music online, take a look at the facts, and you won't wonder any longer.

For the artist, musician, or crafter, there are several distinct advantages to establishing a presence in the online marketplace. For one, you have the ability to reach a global marketplace. According to the International Telecommunication Union, there were 3.2 billion Internet users in 2015 alone, and those numbers continue to rise. That means you can potentially reach millions of people who might be interested in purchasing your creative pieces. Secondly, you can reach them for a fraction of the advertising cost that it would take to reach an audience anywhere else.

FAST FACT

In 2015, online art sales reached $3.27 billion, which was an increase in 24% from the previous year. If the online art market continues to grow at this rate, the online art market will reach $9.58 billion by 2020.[1]

---

1. Weinswig, 2016.

For example, if you ran a small newspaper ad to sell your creative works, who would see it? They would be local customers, not worldwide customers. And that small sized single ad alone could cost you at least $50-$100 just for a one week run. Now imagine a website that is dedicated to selling your creative works and that could potentially reach billions of people and may only cost a few hundred dollars for the full year.

What's also great about the Internet is that you can sell your works much more quickly, since you have a greater audience that can see your work just as soon as you post it. Let's take a closer look.

The Benefits of Online Sales Over Traditional Methods

Let's consider two artists: One artist, preferring the traditional method of selling his or her artworks, submits proposals to art gallery owners, enters works into local and regional art shows, and develops print advertising to reach potential customers. The other, understanding the power of the Internet to market and sell artworks, develops and implements a marketing plan based on a business website, online auctions, networking with other online artists, and regular email promotions.

The traditional marketer will spend a considerable amount of time writing query letters (proposals) to art galleries, filling out entry forms for upcoming art shows, developing print marketing—flyers, postcards, press releases, and business cards—which all cost money too. For all this effort, they reach a relatively small audience—those who see their advertisements, those who wander through the galleries where the artwork hang, and those who attend the art shows where the art has (hopefully) been accepted.

FAST FACT

92 percent of online art buyers said they would buy another piece of art online within the next 12 months.[2]

The online marketer will also spend a substantial amount of time developing marketing materials—such as an attractive and easily navigable website, artwork photographs and descriptions, promotional articles, weblog posts, Twitter posts, and more. Unlike the traditional marketing artist, they will have the opportunity to show their artwork to not just hundreds or even thousands of people, but to literally millions of potential customers all over the world.

Aside from the ability to reach millions of potential buyers each day, having a global presence online gives a working artist a few other key advantages as well.

---

2. Cain & Kaplan, 2016.

The Internet never closes

An artist marketing their creative works on-line does not have to deal with the constraints of typical gallery or studio hours. Artwork can be purchased online any time of the day or night, and the artist does not even have to be in front of the computer to complete the sale. This means that while an online marketing artist sleeps, both night owls and people halfway across the world can buy their art.

People have different tastes in art

When an artist markets through a gallery in a local area, he or she is limited by the tastes, attitudes, and opinions of the local culture. For example, if you paint artworks that draw influence from surrealism, but the local community is primarily interested in realism, you likely will not have much success marketing your artworks locally. You will need to either change the style and subject matter of your artwork or be content with enjoying your artwork in your own home.

When you market via the Internet, you are not constrained by the tastes and preferences of the local art-buying public. Your artwork *will* appeal to someone, and that person may be in the next town over or several time zones away.

A global audience creates more opportunities to reach different types of buyers

An artist in his or her hometown may be limited to a certain type of buyers for creative works, such as homeowners looking for artwork display in a residence or individual buyers seeking to purchase a CD for personal use. While these certainly represent viable markets for an artist, they are not the only ones that can benefit from access to creative works.

A global presence gives an artist access not only to individuals, but also to small businesses looking for artwork to display in office waiting rooms or corporations seeking large works to display in lobbies, company cafeterias, boardrooms, and employee work areas. Similarly, the worldwide presence available through Internet marketing gives someone like a musician the opportunity to attract clients who are looking for music to use in advertisements and other promotional materials.

Selling online minimizes advertising costs

As mentioned earlier, when marketing online, you can reach a large number of potential customers with a much smaller advertising cost than if you marketed to customers offline. Online advertising can be a cost-effective way to reach the people who want to buy your artworks, crafts, photographs, and music. With traditional marketing of creative works, an artist can spend a significant amount of money on the design, printing, and distribution of business cards, postcards, flyers, and other printed marketing materials.

In addition, some art galleries charge hanging fees or display fees for each piece of artwork placed on display in the gallery. Craft malls also charge fees for the rental of the space necessary to display craft items.

These fees do not include gallery commission amounts that are charged against the sale of each artwork that finds a buyer through a gallery. The gallery commissions are a percentage of the sale price of each artwork or craft item—this can be as much of 50 percent in some galleries.

It's easy to spend thousands of dollars building your presence in brick-and-mortar galleries with no guarantee you will be able to make the money back through the sale of your creative works.

Let us compare this with marketing your creative works online. The cost of registering the domain name for your website is typically between $10 and $20, and some website hosting providers, such as **www.ibuilt.net**, **www.godaddy.com**, and **www.ixwebhosting.com**, will waive the cost of registering your website's domain name when you purchase a hosting package through them.

The cost of hosting packages varies according to the features the hosting provider offers and the ability the website owner has to customize and update his or her site. Some providers, such as **www.godaddy.com**, offer basic hosting packages that you can purchase for less than eight dollars a month, as well as other hosting packages that include website design software and even professional website design.

Other hosting providers offer more robust website design features, such as the ability to include forms to capture visitor contact information and deliver it to your email inbox—**www.ibuilt.net** offers such services for $19.99 per month, and **www.sitekreator.com** offers a similar service, and more, for $33.29 per month.

Aside from your website, there are various art, craft, and music cooperative sites that you can subscribe to for a nominal fee. For example, **www.ebsqart .com** gives you access to exclusive online art shows, artist community bulletin boards, charity events, and contests for $6.50 per month.

If you are willing to take the time to do some research, you can also utilize pay-per-click (PPC) search engine marketing to help bring customers to your website. Realistically, you can spend as much or as little for this type of advertising as you want, but if you bid on the right keywords (Check Google Ad-Words and Microsoft Big Ads), you can gain exposure for as little as five cents per click. You, as the advertiser, pay the publisher when the ad is clicked on.

There are also marketing techniques you can implement for free, such as writing online blogs, participating in discussion board threads, writing articles for online directories, building links to your website, and optimizing the content of your website so it will appear high in the rankings of search engines such as Google, MSN, Yahoo!, and others. Chapter 3 of this book will discuss these techniques in more detail.

It is possible to build a well-crafted online marketing strategy for less than $100 per month — even less if you are willing to do some of the work involved in creating your own website and optimizing it for high search engine rankings. You would be hard pressed to develop an effective advertising strategy for this amount in the traditional offline marketing world, but it's possible online.

Selling online moves your artwork quickly

Art galleries, craft malls, and music stores move works rather slowly, partially because of the lack of significant daily traffic through the gallery's doors and partially because people tend to just browse when they visit a gallery. Unless they are displaying your works entirely on consignment, art gallery owners and craft mall owners are not particularly motivated to sell your art, because you are already paying them for the privilege of displaying your creative works in their retail spaces.

When you sell your creative works online, you are in better control of how quickly you sell your art. It may take time to build a steady stream of traffic for your website, but there are several ways you can use the Internet to achieve impressive sales while you are building a loyal customer base online.

The first way is through using online art auctions, which we will discuss further in Chapters 6, 7, and 8. Sometimes you will find buyers have placed bids on an artwork before the paint is even dry, so to speak.

Another way that online marketing can help you enjoy frequent sales as an artist is by allowing you to display more artworks on a single website than you ever could in a physical gallery. More choice means more sales.

A third way you can use the Internet to increase the speed and frequency of your sales is by displaying your artwork in many different places at one time. You can display it on your website, in an online auction, on your blog, on an artist's cooperative website such as **www.deviantart.com**, and in discussion board postings (if permitted by the discussion board moderator).

Can You Make Enough Money Selling Art Online?

Yes, and millions do! Actually, more people are buying artwork online than anywhere else, including at art galleries, art festivals, and art shows. The online art market is estimated be growing about 20 percent per year. Selling your work online is actually called "E-Commerce," or the transaction of buying or selling online. And if you are wondering how big the E-Commerce business is, it's probably bigger than you would ever imagine.

FAST FACT

In 2016, 79 percent of online art buyers spend less than $5,000 on an art piece.[3]

---

3. Read, 2016.

According to Ever Merchant, every 30 seconds, more than $1.2 million is generated over Internet sales. Amazon, eBay, Pinterest, and more are all raking in the big money. That's money that you can be tapping into by selling your artwork. According to the United States Department of Labor, the median salary for an artist, including painters, sculptors and illustrators, is $46,460 (May 2015). This number could be greatly increased with your Internet sales.

What Art is Being Sold Online?

If you can create a work of art, you can pretty much sell it online. Whether it's sterling silver jewelry, original oil paintings, digital art, fashion photography, metal sculptures, or glass vases, it can be sold online.

Finding Your Online Niche

The good part of online marketing is that many sales are being conducted over the Internet these days. That bad part is that there is a lot of competition out there. However, everyone's creativity is different, so you likely have your very own look to begin with.

Here are a few things to keep in mind: Remember that with any piece of art, there should be a concept, a motivation, and a purpose. Find your own style and look and do the best you can with it. Focus in on doing one or two things well over being all over the map with your art. Study the great artists and the movements, analyze them, and take an art history class if you can. It's important to understand yourself as an artist and understand the artists who came before you as art builds on itself through the generations.

Once you have found and developed your own personal style that you want to market, try showing it to friends and family, art lovers, and art teachers to get feedback. Search online art galleries or places like **www.youtube.com**, **www.reddit.com/r/music**, or **www.spotify.com** and see what is popular and what is selling. Then reflect on why the work of art is doing so well. Is it the topic? The style? The medium? The price? All of these things should be considered.

Once you have a work of art that is ready to sell, whether it's landscape paintings or handmade jewelry or a cool tune, remember that your online presence should reflect the style of what you are selling. If you are creating colorful landscapes, then your website, blog, or Facebook page should stylistically fit with it. The style should be cohesive so that when a potential customer sees your online presence, it has a similar look to it. The word is called "branding" and it is the look, style and feel of your product and yourself.

If you think of a product like Nike or McDonalds, everything they put out in the public looks like their brand — the Nike swish and the golden arches are everywhere. The same goes with all of your marketing materials, including business cards or brochures. They should look like your online presence. These printed pieces can be designed and ordered online from places like **www.vistaprint.com** or **www.avery.com.** Remember, even though this book focuses on selling online, it doesn't hurt to try the traditional means along with it or have a few business cards in your back pocket for networking purposes. We will discuss more about this in Chapter 2.

Now that you know *why* you should be selling your creative works online, let us move on to the next chapter of this book, which will cover the first topic of learning *how* to successfully sell your works online—selecting the right hardware, software, and support for your online business.

CHAPTER 2

What You Will Need to Sell Your Products Online

This chapter will outline the basic components you will need to launch your Internet business. We'll also cover what you need to get started in terms of building and maintaining your brand, and we'll go over some of the nuts and bolts of the financial considerations of owning an online business.

Your Computer

You likely already own a computer. However, if you don't, it's time to consider purchasing one for your online business. Even a laptop will do. If you can't afford a computer, you might try a smartphone, a tablet, or a notebook, but make sure you check out the capabilities before you make a purchase. You may need to scan, upload images, record video and all kinds of tasks for your online business, which may take a heavy-duty system with a fast processing speed and a large storage capacity.

Whatever system you work with, it is a good idea to evaluate its performance to ensure it can handle the tasks you need it to.

Here is what you will need to consider with a computer:

Hard drive

This is the component of your computer where your images, documents, music files, and software files are stored. The capacity of a hard drive is expressed in megabytes (MB), gigabytes (GB), or terabytes (TB).

Currently, internal hard drives are available with storage capacities ranging from 320 GB to 6.0 TB+. A megabyte is 1 million bytes, a gigabyte is 1 billion bytes, and a terabyte is 1 trillion bytes. The larger the storage capacity of your computer's hard drive, the more expensive it will be. However, when storing music, digital files, or digital movies, you might need a lot of space.

Also, remember that the programs and or applications you install take up space too. For example, a program like Photoshop takes up about 3 GB on your hard drive. And Adobe Acrobat Reader DC (which allows you to open and view PDF files) will occupy 154.6 MB, while Dreamweaver CC (a software application that allows you to design your own websites) takes up nearly 324 GB of space.

Then there are the file sizes of what you created with the software. They take up space too. Here are two examples to help put things in perspective:

- A 10-page, text-only document written in Microsoft Word will occupy roughly 50 kilobytes (KB) of space—that is 0.00005 GB. This means you could save 100,000 pages of text to your hard drive and still only take up 1 GB of disk space.

- A high-resolution image that measures 1,000 pixels x 1,600 pixels will take up between 1 megabyte (MB) and 3 MB of disk space. This means you can store between 300 and 1,000 images of this size and resolution on 1 GB of your hard drive's disk space.

If you plan on designing your own website using graphics software such as Adobe Photoshop or Corel Paint Shop Pro, or storing large amounts of photo images on your computer, you should look for a computer with at least an 80 GB hard drive, which is considered "common use." Choosing an even larger hard drive, such as a 150 GB or even a 300 GB drive, can help ensure you will not have to upgrade your computer for several years.

If it is in your budget, it is also a good idea to purchase an external hard drive to back up all your image, text, and software files so you don't lose them if your computer crashes or gets corrupted with a virus.

Memory card

A memory card is an internal computer component that provides RAM (Random Access Memory) to run the processes on your computer, such as your operating system, software applications, Internet Explorer windows, and maintenance applications, such as virus scanners and anti-spyware programs.

The power of memory cards is expressed in MB or GB. The more power your memory card has, the faster your processes will run and the more processes you can run at the same time. At least a 2 GB or even a 16 GB memory card is recommended to run the processes on your computer, especially when you are running multiple programs simultaneously. You don't want your computer to freeze up.

Processor

A computer's processor unit (or CPU) acts as the gateway for all your computer's functions. As its name suggests, it is responsible for processing all the data used to make your audio, video, and software applications run smoothly. It is really the brain of your computer.

There are two main manufacturers of computer processors today: Intel and AMD. Intel processors are the most commonly used in personal computers. They are sold as packages through vendors like Dell and Gateway, Inc.

If your business building tasks will be limited to simple web design and image uploading, and you do not mind slightly slower processing speeds, you can get away with using a slower, less expensive processor. If, on the other hand, you will be using graphics programs such as Photoshop or Paint Shop Pro or using video or other multimedia to enhance your business website, make sure you invest in a processor that will give you the speed and power you need to handle these applications.

CD-ROM, CD-RW, DVD-R drive, or flash drive

To install software onto your computer, you will need to have at least a CD-ROM drive, however, some software, such as Adobe Photoshop can be purchased (outright or by the month), and then downloaded directly to your system via **www.adobe.com**.

If you plan to use more than one computer for your business building activities, it's a good idea to have a CD-RW drive, which will allow you to copy files to a blank disk so you can transfer the files from one computer to another. An even more versatile option is a DVD-R drive, which will allow you to create DVDs of movies showcasing your works, video artist biographies, and other promotional materials. However, you can also use a USB flash drive. Some flash drives offer up to 256 GB of storage, or even more.

Video card (or graphics card)

This is the component of your computer that acts as an interface between your computer and your display monitor, generating video images that can be displayed on the system's monitor. When you have a good video card, your computer will display higher-quality images and play video files more smoothly.

The capacity of a video card to handle images and streaming video is expressed in GB — this refers to the video file size that a video card can process at any given time without tapping into the computer's RAM or memory.

It's a good idea to purchase a computer with at least a 2 GB or, better yet, 4 GB video card — this will give you the image quality you need to enhance photographs to display on your website, online auctions, and blogs.

Sound card

This is the computer component that acts as an interface between your computer and external sound output devices, such as computer speakers or a stereo system. The better the quality your sound card is, the better the quality of the audio output from your speakers will be.

If you are a musician who will be selling your songs online, a high-quality sound card is essential, because it allows you to make sure your uploaded music files are as clear and balanced as possible. Plus, it also optimizes your use of music-mixing software, which will allow you to adjust the various levels of your recording, edit parts of your songs, and create remixes of popular song tracks.

Computer packages

The easiest way to purchase a computer that meets all your needs for running a successful online business is to purchase a computer package from one of the many online or offline vendors that specialize in creating and selling packaged units designed to fit specific budgets and applications.

The advantages of purchasing a packaged computer system are threefold. First, you will not have to find and price each individual component of your computer separately and make sure that they are compatible with one another. Second, purchasing a packaged computer can save you a substantial amount of money over purchasing individual components. Third, you will not have to assemble the computer yourself or pay someone to come to your home and assemble it for you.

A variety of computer packages designed to meet nearly any user's needs are available through **www.dell.com** or **www.gateway.com**. These websites offer several configurations for both desktop and laptop computers, and you can customize your computer package to add, remove, or upgrade components before your computer is built. (Watch for specials, such as upgrades, that change weekly.) If you prefer a Mac, try **www.apple.com**.

Keep in mind that, while the prices of the low-end packages are attractive, they may not provide you with the power or speed that you need to run your online business.

Your Peripherals

Now let's look at the peripheral devices that will help you build your online business.

Video monitor

Purchasing a high-quality monitor will go a long way toward helping you create and view images of your artwork, handmade crafts, and photographs. After all, these images help your creative come to life on a potential customer's computer screen. They must be clear, undistorted, and free of distracting shadows and glare. Otherwise, they won't sell well.

A large, high quality monitor will help you spot flaws in these images and will be indispensable for using image enhancement programs that allow for image enhancing and editing, such as Adobe Photoshop, TruView, Photo-Flair, or AutoFX.

Digital camera

Purchasing a digital camera is important to creating images that will help sell your artwork. However, many smartphones have high res digital capacities that produce high resolution, large megabytes (MB) images. However, they may not have all that a digital camera offers in terms of capabilities, like using long lenses or even a flash.

Here are a few things to look for in a digital camera:

- *High megapixel capacity.* When you enlarge the pictures, your photo software needs to have sufficiently detailed information to reproduce the image accurately in larger sizes. Without a high megapixel capacity, your software will pixelate the image — that is, turn areas of your image into visibly noticeable blocks of color rather than reproducing a true image. To create accurate, detailed images of your creative works that can be enlarged to 800 x 1200 pixels or larger, you will need a digital camera with no less than a 6-megapixel capacity. Cameras are now available even higher megapixel capacity, which can produce images that cannot only be used in online marketing, but also flyers and posters for offline marketing as well. However, the higher the megapixel, the higher the price.

- *Optical zoom.* Nearly every digital camera today has a zoom feature that lets you take close-up shots without actually moving closer to the subject you are photographing. When you are shopping for a digital camera, it is important to note whether a particular model features *optical* zoom or *digital* zoom.

Digital zoom crops and enlarges an image digitally, which can cause the same sort of pixilation that occurs when you enlarge a low-resolution image on your computer. Optical zoom, on the other hand, works by physically distancing the lenses within the camera, much like a traditional 35 mm film camera. This allows you to create a close-up image that is undistorted and free from the pixilation caused by digital zoom features. Some cameras have both optical zoom and digital zoom features.

- *Point and shoot functionality.* Complicated cameras with numerous manual functions are fine for the true photography enthusiast, but for the purpose of creating images as marketing tools, you might want idea to stick with point and shoot models that will allow you to photograph your creative works quickly and easily.

There are many great digital cameras on the market, and a good way to start looking for one is by reading the reviews. Try **www.cnet.com, www .pcmag.com**, or **www.techradar.com**.

Video camera

Although embedded video is by no means a required element, it's a great way to keep your website visitors around longer so they will be more likely to purchase from you. Many smartphones have video cameras built in and many digital cameras also have video capacities.

Audio speakers

If you are a visual artist, a standard set of speakers, such as the ones packaged with average quality desktop computers, will serve you just fine. If you are an online musician, though, a high-quality set of speakers is indispensable. Again, you might first check the reviews before making a purchase. Here are a few good places to start: **www.digitaltrends.com** or **www.pcmag.com**.

Printer

Your printer will likely be used primarily to print invoices, contracts, shipping labels, and other documents related to the sale or commission of creative works. A simple, inexpensive inkjet printer will perform well for this purpose. They run as little as $80-$100.

Scanner

For artwork and photographs less than 8.5" x 11" in size, a simple flatbed scanner is ideal and may work better than taking pictures with your camera and uploading them. A flatbed scanner has a large glass plate on which pictures are placed for scanning and a flat-hinged lid that holds the picture against the glass to prevent curling or ripples. The result is a clean, neatly centered image that makes your artwork stand out. Many printers have built in scanning capacities.

Your Internet Service Provider

To build an online business, you will need a reliable Internet connection. Internet service providers (ISP) offer several packages to meet your needs with prices that depend on the type and speed of the connection you choose.

High-speed Internet packages cost at least $30 to $70 per month.

If you are using a laptop or smartphone for your online business, you can use a wireless Internet card to connect to the Internet at stores and restaurants designated as Wi-Fi Hotspots without an Internet package of your own. If you have a desktop computer in your home that already has a high-speed Internet connection, you can access the Internet on your laptop by connecting a router (a device that permits an Internet connection to laptops in or near your home) to your desktop computer.

You can also purchase a wireless Internet card for your laptop that allows online access through satellite transmission of Internet data — this allows you to connect from virtually anywhere, regardless of whether a standard wireless connection is available. Check with your Internet service provider.

Now that we have discussed the nuts and bolts of what you need to consider for your system, let's talk about what you need to also think about before you launch your business.

Developing Your Brand

Before you rush out and open an Etsy shop, build a website, or try your hand at a blog, you want to first establish a look, style, and feel that is all your own. Consistency is a key word here as you want both your online and your offline presence to be similar enough that your customers can recognize it. Here are a few things to think about:

FAST FACT

In 2016, 79 percent of people said they wanted more background information on the artist and the piece.[4]

---

4. Read, 2016.

Establishing a name and a look

What will you call your business? Annie's Artwork? Inspired Visions? Find a name that resonates with you. Think of something that is catchy and memorable or at least fits with what you are selling. Use a thesaurus to find new words. Also, search the Internet to make sure that no one else is using the same name. If so, change it. You don't want to infringe on someone else's trademarked name or run into legal entanglements.

Additionally, you might also try a search at the US Patent and Trademark Office at: **https://www.uspto.gov/trademarks-application-process/search -trademark-database**. You might also want to register your business name, which can be done at your county clerk's office or with your state's government office, depending on which state you reside in.

CASE STUDY: KRISTEN QUEEN

kristenqueenart@yahoo.com

In my experience as a customer I find the ease, convenience, and audience of online sales is what encouraged me to further pursue the idea of moving my artwork online. Though it will never replace physically going to a venue, or gallery where artwork is showcased; it provides the overall convenience that many of us in today's hectic society can more easily work with based on our changing schedules.

Having only recently taken my artistic skills to a more professional level, I realized that in order to be profitable and reputable you need resources that can provide such opportunities. The Internet can readily provide multiple opportunities to both the emerging and seasoned artist gathering from the multiple artists I have spoken with. It is conducive to my schedule, and time.

Even with a change in the market demand, artwork is still alive and well on the Internet. Where as local galleries were having a difficult task moving pieces out and bringing new works in, Internet sales from EBay to personal web pages and professional galleries online were doing well.

Online sales provide more direct means of your net profit. Marketing your artwork from a personal website removes the hassle associated with "middle men" concerning gallery brokers, agents, and other physical aspects of making your art accessible to the most inclined market; to include the hassle of transporting artwork, hanging artwork, all while according to someone else's schedule and commission fees.

While there are many art agents online that will charge you accordingly, I believe that a personal website and a successful marketing strategy is all one will need to be moderately successful in online sales. This is a very simple and realistic goal that is very appealing to someone like me.

In order to keep things more fresh and organized I am hoping to launch my website by the first of the year. I am looking at using SiteKreator as my web hosting service. Their website has a very attractive layout with online demos, archives of page samples, and free trials. Most web hosting services do not provide this level of interest when attracting potential customers. SiteKreator although unintentionally has become synonymous with online art based websites. They have done well to encourage that marketing niche. Being 'artist friendly' is a plus for me. This means that galleries, perspective clients, and other artists are now more accessible then ever to each other. Online sales is all about networking; any additional intrinsic qualities pertaining to my specific market that a web host can offer is something crucial to consider.

For my site I want to keep it simple, classy but interesting and not too formal. The viewer should be concerned with the artwork. I look at it in this way, if I were driving past a building with an understated, boring, or poorly kept shop front I would not stop. If it was too over the top, and cheesy I would not stop. Even though either one may have EXACTLY what I was looking for, but the first impression is what sells first! You have to sell the idea and the place before you sell the item inside.

Consider colors, fonts, and images

Are there a few colors that fit with what you are selling? Are there colors you like? Do they look good with the name of your business? Are they easy to see online? Or might they look too saturated or too faded? Find a couple of colors and stick with them for your look and style. Also, use the same font throughout your online presence. Find a font that is easy to read and looks good with the title of your business. You might consider either using a different font for the title of your business or creating a logo or design that you will use again and again, such as the Nike swish.

The same goes with the accent images that you might use on your website or blog. Unless they are your own images that you created, make sure you are not using them improperly. Many images have copyrights and cannot be used without permission. If in doubt, don't use anything that isn't your own creation. There are some websites that offer free images, such as **https://pixabay.com**, **www.freeimages.com**, or **www.unsplash.com**.

Finding Out About the Financials

Although we will discuss more about the financial considerations in Chapter 11, it's important to have some idea of what you need to keep track of before you even launch your website — things like inventory, income and expenses, as well as costs and tax considerations.

Keeping track of inventory, income, expenses, and business banking

If your business is small enough, you could get a notebook and write down all of your income, expenses, and inventory (or have a notebook for each). However, there are software programs like QuickBooks or Wave that will help you keep track of everything from computer expenses to art materials. Also, if you don't already have a bank account, now might be a good time to open one up. It's a good place to keep your money once your online business starts making money. If you are underage, you might qualify for a free juvenile account at your parents' bank. Either way, you will get a monthly statement that shows all of your funds that came in and all that went out.

When looking for a bank, be sure to shop around. Some banks have high monthly fees, and you may need to keep a certain balance from month to month. There's also PayPal, where you can accept online payments and keep funds in your account. Mostly, it's important to keep an organized record of everything. Save your receipts!

Taxes and financial questions

If you earn an income, you likely have to complete your taxes every year. And if you have earned little, you will likely get all the money you paid in taxes back in the form of a refund. However, if you start making a lot of money with your Internet sales, you might have earned enough that you have to pay in. This is why it is so important to keep track of everything, including expenses — art materials, computer hardware and software, pens and paper, gas mileage, and more — that can be deducted against your income if it is related directly to your business.

You can find out more about taxes by seeking the advice of a tax professional, or checking with the Internal Revenue Service (IRS) directly at **www.irs.gov**. The Small Business Administration also has a wealth of information on their website, such as How to Start a Business, Registering a Business Name, and Obtaining a Business License at **www.sba.gov**.

CHAPTER 3

Creating a Website

The next step is to create a website to serve as the hub of your business. When you have the correct tools, and the know-how, it is easy to build and maintain an attractive, easily navigable website that will compel your visitors to purchase your artworks, craft items, photographs, or music.

This chapter will give you the information you need to build a website, and help you learn how to reserve a name for your website, how to use templates to make your website building process quick and efficient, and how to make your website easy to navigate so your visitors can find the items they want to purchase.

There are several reasons having a dedicated website for your online business is essential:

- *It establishes your credibility as an artist and a businessperson.* Having a website shows you are serious about your career as an artist, musician, craftsperson, or photographer. It demonstrates a sense of professionalism. It also assures customers that they will be able to purchase your works and contact you with questions and commission requests.

- *It gives your customers the ability to purchase from your selections quickly and easily.* A website gives visitors the opportunity to choose and purchase items from your entire body of work, all while enjoying a simple process to do so.

- *It increases your repeat business.* Once a customer has made a purchase from your website, he or she will likely come back again, especially if you are frequently changing content on your website and giving them a reason to return and possibly buy again. (More about adding content in Chapter 4 and Chapter 12.)

- *It is one of the least expensive forms of online advertising available.* If you are willing to design the website yourself, you may be able to do it for under $50. Once it's finished and uploaded, there are several free and low-cost ways to promote your website.

With these reasons in mind, let us get started building your website!

Your Domain Name

Before you begin building your website, you will need a domain name for your website. A domain name is the address that an Internet user types to access a particular website. For example, **www.jello.com**. Choosing a domain name is a tricky process; because it should reflect your personality as an artist, photographer, or musician while being easy to remember. Not only that, but it must also be a domain name that is not already in use or registered to another person or business.

Using your name as your domain name works well if you already have an established following, but if you are new to the world of the Internet and do not have an offline client base that will visit your website, this is not the best way to attract visitors. If you want to use your name in your website address, it's best to use it in conjunction with other short words or phrases that accurately describe your business. For example, if John Smith wanted to build a website for his photography studio, **www.johnsmithphotography.com** would be a good choice for him to attract website visitors while also building name recognition on the Internet.

A good way to test out domain names and determine whether they are available is to visit **www.godaddy.com**. There is a domain search function on GoDaddy's homepage where you can enter potential domain names to check for availability. If a particular domain name is already taken, GoDaddy will suggest alternate domain names that are available.

Even if your domain name is available with an extension other than .com, such as .biz, .info, or .tv, it is important that you select a domain name with a .com extension, as that is considered more professional.

Once you have selected a domain name, you can purchase and register it through **www.godaddy.com** or through hundreds of other hosting providers, such as **www.domains.google**.

The cost of registering a domain name varies among hosting providers, but you can expect to pay less than $20 per year to reserve and use a domain name. If you purchase a hosting package and register a domain name with the same hosting provider, you may be able to obtain a domain name at a reduced cost. An action like this costs under $10 year through places like GoDaddy. Hosts such as **www.ixwebhosting.com** will give you three free domain name registrations when you buy a hosting package that supports up to 15 websites for $7.95 per month. This can be a useful proposition if you create several different types of artwork or if you create not only artwork, but crafts and photography as well. You can also get free domain name registration through **www.ibuilt.net**, although the hosting packages are more expensive ($19.95 to 39.95 per month) because they offer more features.

CASE STUDY: LYNNE TAETZSCH

ARTBYLT.COM
3 Snyder Heights
Ithaca, NY 14850
607-273-0266
Lynne@ARTBYLT.COM

I have always enjoyed working with computers as a user, not a programmer, and when I saw artists beginning to put their art on Web sites back in 1998, I decided to make one for my art. I began using the Netscape "composer" tool which came with that browser then in order to put together a simple Web site with my paintings on it. At that time I used to photograph my paintings with an SLR camera outdoors to make slides. Instead, I had color prints made and then scanned them with a flatbed scanner in order to get the digital images for the Web site.

Over the years I continued to revise my Web site and to upgrade to more complex software for building it. For a few years I used "Hotdog," which taught me a lot about html code. Finally, a few years ago I bought "Dreamweaver" and took a class in how to use it. I also use a digital camera now to photograph the paintings, and a flatbed scanner for drawings. I still do all my own design, coding, upgrading, promotion, etc., for my Web site.

In 2000, I made my first sales from the Web site. Sales were very slow at first, but have gradually increased over the years.

I make 90% of my sales online. The rest are through galleries, word-of-mouth, and the Greater Ithaca Art Trail open studio weekends.

I have an art blog called *All About Art*, and for the last six months I've been making a drawing and writing about it every day in the art blog. Writing regularly increases readership. I also have a few videos on YouTube. I do not do auctions or e-bay, but I am listed in some online group art sites. I've sold a couple paintings that way and do get some traffic from them.

My Web site has been the ultimate tool in establishing my presence online. It takes a lot of work, but it is definitely worth it. Not only do I make direct sales from it, but I hear from gallery owners, art consultants and interior designers. I also get email from other artists all over the world and have made many artist friends that way.

It took a couple of years before I made my first sale, but I think today that wouldn't be the case. Back then, people were not as comfortable buying anything over the Internet, no less fine art. There are still many people who will not buy a piece of art unless they see it in person, but there are enough who will, and that number keeps growing. The important thing is to offer a money-back guarantee and to have a secure method for placing an order.

Some customers want to know the exact shade of red or green in a painting before they will buy it. In this case, I offer to send a printed photo of the work, which has helped to finalize sales. Every once in a while I come upon a difficult client who wants a better price, a Saturday delivery, or something else that costs me time, money and aggravation. I have learned a lot over the years from dealing with problem customers like these. I've lost some sales and money, but the lessons have been invaluable.

I enjoy being able to reach people all over the world, and having them love and praise my art. A gallery audience is limited to the people who walk in, but the Internet offers the possibility of unlimited worldwide exposure.

I also enjoy "talking" to people through the words I put on my Web site, as well as email exchanges. It gives clients a chance to get to know me and my art without having to come to a gallery reception to meet me.

The Internet is great for networking, and I have met many artists this way. We all help and encourage each other, and I've learned so much from them.

Your Hosting Provider

A hosting provider is a company that places your website files on its servers (computers that hold a very large amount of information) and allows visitors to access your website through its servers. It is essentially a place where you go to rent out your web space. A few of the more popular hosting providers are: **www.godaddy.com**, **www.hostmonster.com**, **https://otherpeoplespixels.com**, **www.vistaprint.com**, **www.weebly.com**, **www.sitebuilder.com**, **www.websitebuilder.com**, **www.wix.com**, **www .ehost.com**, **www.shopify.com**, and **www.wordpress.com**.

When choosing a hosting provider for your website, there are a number of things you should consider:

- *Storage space for your files.* As a person selling creative works online, you will be uploading numerous files to your website, such as images of your artwork, music files, and downloadable text files. If you are building a more robust website that includes Flash animation or video files, those will be stored on your hosting provider's servers as well. Therefore, adequate space is important.

  Hosting providers differ greatly in the amount of file storage space they will allow per account. Three hosting packages that are available from **www.godaddy.com** provide 100 MB and even unlimited amounts of storage space. Other hosting providers, such as **www.hostmonster.com**, offer a variety of hosting options and spaces.

- *File transfer allowance.* File transfer refers to the process of temporarily uploading the files that comprise your website to a visitor's Internet browser. If a visitor accesses a webpage that contains ten photographs that are 2 MB in size each, the file transfer size of those photographs is 20 MB. If the visitor visits ten similar pages on your website, 200 MB of your file transfer allowance are used.

- *Personalized email addresses.* If you operate a website that sells creative works and a customer requests additional information or asks about a purchase via email, he or she would rather receive a response from yourname@yourwebsite.com than from a free account such as Gmail, Yahoo, or Hotmail. Having an email address that corresponds with your website address looks more professional. Some web-hosting providers, such as www. godaddy.com, https://otherpeoplespixels.com, and even **www.vistaprint.com**, include a free mail with the purchase of a package.

- *Site design software.* If you do not know HTML (the language in which websites are written) or you have never created a website before and do not want to spend much time designing it, you can use site design software offered by some hosting providers.

The type of website design software provided by website hosting companies allows you to choose from a collection of templates and then fill pre-set areas with text, images, video files, and links to other websites. The amount of control you have to customize and the overall design of the templates varies; but the more control you have over the overall look and feel of your website, the more expensive the hosting package will be.

Look for a hosting provider that provides a demo of their design software; a video demo will give you a basic idea of how to use the software to create your site. Some offer a limited free trial period to let you test out the software.

- *CGI forms (Common Gateway Interface).* These are areas of a website where a visitor fills in his or her personal data to get more information about a product or to subscribe to a website's newsletter or email list. When a visitor fills out a form and clicks the "Submit" button, the form sends the information to a program on the hosting company's server that translates the information into a format that can be sent to you via email or used to populate a database.

You can use the information you collect from these forms to build an email list, which you can use to periodically contact your website visitors to notify them of new artwork, crafts, or music when it becomes available and to let them know about sales and special promotions. We will discuss more about this in Chapter 9.

Building Your Website

The remainder of this chapter will give you tips and ideas for creating a website that is easy to navigate, is visually appealing to your visitors, and nets you the most sales.

Whether you use a template offered by a website design host (easier) or you use an advanced website building software package, such as *Microsoft Expression Web 4* (formerly Microsoft FrontPage) or *Adobe Dreamweaver CC* (harder), the first goal of building your business site should be to create a website that has a clean design and is easy to navigate.

Here are the essential pages of an art-, craft-, or music-based website:

1. *The Home Page.* This is the first page that most people will see when they visit your website. For this reason, designing an effective home page is particularly important, because it will be your only tool to attract the attention of website visitors and make them want to explore the other pages of your site. Your home page should focus on your art, not on your career as an artist or the professional logo you may have created for your art business.

   Also, make sure that links to your other pages are easy to find on your home page and throughout your website. The longer your visitors stay on your website, the more likely they are to buy from you — and letting

them see your best work as soon as your site loads is the best way to make your visitors want to stay.

2. *A Gallery of Your Creative Works.* Aside from an effective home page, your gallery page is the best way to keep visitors on your site. Your gallery page should not include any extraneous images, text, or animation — this is a place for your visitors to focus solely on the works you have for sale.

    Multiple gallery pages are fine if your artwork, crafts, or photographs can be easily divided into different categories. Just do not make your visitors click through too many website pages to find the creative works they are looking for.

    If you have several gallery pages, one way to help streamline the navigation for your visitors is to build a gallery front page listing all your different art categories with a sample image of each type of artwork for each category. You can even make the images link to your separate gallery pages, in addition to having the category descriptions link to the pages.

3. *A Biography Page.* Your website visitors will naturally want to know more about you. This page lets your visitors know who you are, how you were drawn to the creative arts, and what you hope to convey through your works. The biography page should also include your photograph so your visitors can see the artist behind the work.

4. *The Contact Page.* This page should invite your visitors to contact you with questions, comments, and requests. You can also state your basic terms for commissioned works, so that people interested in hiring you to create a custom work will know whether you are available to create commissioned pieces and will understand your fee structure.

    If your website hosting provider supports CGI (it's best if they do), creating a simple CGI form on this page is the best way for your website visitors to contact you. This form lets your visitors know what informa-

tion you need to provide a response and cuts down on the number of unfocused and incomplete messages you receive in your email inbox.

There are other pages you can add to your website, such as Frequently Asked Questions, Links (to other websites or your online auctions), and Recently Sold works. These pages help add content to your website, giving your visitors more to look at, but they are not essential to creating a website that will sell.

Once you have decided on these topics, you are ready to design the website itself.

Color

Instead of using a texture or an image as your background, stick to a plain colored background that contrasts with the color of your text so viewers can easily read the content of your website. A simple white, grey, or light blue background works well with black text. If you want to use a darker background, such as black or navy blue, use white text to tell viewers about your creative works.

Also, make sure you use the same background and text colors for each page on your website. This will ensure that your site is consistent and not distracting from your work. Keep in mind that colors look different on every computer monitor and laptop screen, so, if you are having difficulty deciding between a background and text color combination that is aesthetically pleasing and one that contrasts well, choose contrasting colors.

FAST FACT

In 2016, 73 percent of people said they would like to talk to the artist before buying a piece of art online.[5]

Text

When designing your website, make sure the text is easy to find and read. As noted above, the color of your text should contrast with the color of your background. Avoid font sizes and styles that make your text difficult to read.

Also, try to avoid multiple columns of text on a webpage. It is easier for the human eye to focus on a single column of text rather than multiple columns of text on a website. If you must use multiple columns, limit your webpages to two columns so that your website visitors will have a focal point to visually anchor their eyes.

One exception to the one column guideline is the sidebar. Sidebars are narrow vertical boxes that provide information you want to feature prominently on your site. These usually have a background that is different from the rest of the website. The sidebar can include customer testimonials, links

5. Read, 2016.

to works in progress, or any other information that may not be directly related to the content on your page but that is nevertheless important to your visitors.

Image placement

If possible, your images should be centered horizontally on your webpages between blocks of text. This creates a visual flow that will help your visitors stay focused on the content of your site.

Unless you are creating a gallery page, it is not a good idea to place two or three pictures along a horizontal line. This creates a sense of confusion by providing too many items of equal prominence for your visitors to look at.

Adding Images and Video

Although text is important for attracting and retaining website visitors, images are equally important, as visitors want to see websites filled with visually pleasing images. An art website without images will not retain your visitors for long. People expect the content of an art-related website to be visually creative.

Images and videos help the website visitors feel more connected to the content of the website and to you, the artist behind the works. Oftentimes, purchasing artwork or music is an emotional decision, rather than a rational one, and visual media helps you connect to your visitors' emotions.

Images

Along with images of your artwork, you can also include images of things that inspire you—a hiking trail you walk to gather artistic ideas, a section of your city that gave you an idea for a series of creative works, or anything

that ties into your career and vision as an artist. In addition to a professional headshot of yourself on your biography page, you may also want to include other images of yourself, such as pictures of you in your studio, standing next to one of your favorite pieces, or sitting in an environment that inspires you.

Video

Video content can help generate visitor interest. However, the content does not need to be a well-polished presentation of your work or a professional introduction to your career as an artist. You can set up an inexpensive video camera or even a webcam in your studio and record yourself at work. Although your video does not need to appear professionally produced, as it can offer the human touch, you can use inexpensive video editing software, such as *Apple iMovie* or *Corel VideoStudio Ultimate X9*, to select and compile snippets of video from various stages of the creative process. This way, your visitors can see the creation of an artistic work from start to finish in a short time. Your camera may also offer its own built-in editing software, and some editing software may be included in your computer package.

Generally, a video like this should be limited to two or three minutes in length. Also, a short video of you in your studio, maybe greeting your website visitors and inviting them to explore various areas of your site, can be a good way to generate visitor interest.

Creating Site Maps

You should always include a site map somewhere on your website and provide a link to it on each page of your site. A site map is a document that shows every page and subpage of your website so if your visitors are having difficulty finding what they are looking for on your site, they can refer to

your site map to learn how to navigate to the information or products they are looking for.

Site maps are also helpful for search engines, because they provide a comprehensive list of pages and subpages on your site and provide links to each. This helps ensure that search engine spiders (spiders fetch webpages) can find, crawl, and index each page of your site, so your visitors can easily find and visit your webpages.

Many website creation programs offer a feature that will create a site map for you. If you are using a website creation tool that does not offer this feature, you can create a site map for free at **http://googlesiteranks.net /google-sitemap-generator**. There are a few other sites that can assist, such as **https://support.google.com** and **www.xml-sitemaps.com**.

CHAPTER 4

Search Engines, Maximizing Visitors to Your Website, and Shipping

Chapter 1 touched on the basics of a search engine query, via Google, Bing, or Yahoo, but this section will delve into the details of how a search engine query works and how you can use your knowledge of this process to your advantage.

How results are selected for a search engine query

To make a website more prominent in search engine results, or to appear on earlier pages of a search, the owner (you) will submit a website to various search engines in order to alert the search engine that a new website exists or that it has been updated (you will find out more about this in Chapter 10 and 11).

How this works: The spiders that we discussed earlier report their findings to the search engine's database, where the pages of a website are indexed and each page is ranked among the others for search terms.

A search engine's most basic goal in scanning each website for content is to determine how useful a website would be for an Internet user that types a particular query (word or phrase) into a search engine box.

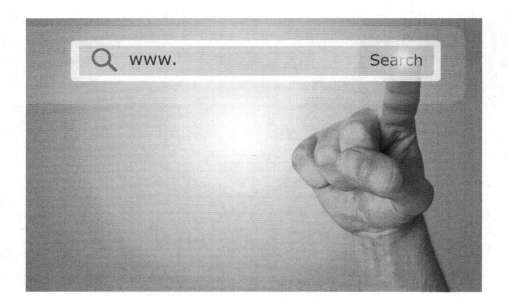

The first page of search results is considered by the search engine to represent the webpages that are the most relevant to what the search engine user is looking for. Getting your webpages into these top ten results will garner substantially more traffic than having your webpages on later pages, because people rarely look at anything after the first two or three pages—either they have found what they are looking for or they modify their search query to try to obtain more relevant results.

Getting Your Website to Rank High in Search Results

Keywords

The most important elements of your content are the keywords. Keywords are, at their most basic level, the terms that an Internet user will type into a search engine query box to obtain webpage results. They include not only single words, but also phrases and common terms that a user would type in to search for webpages.

Before you write a line of website content, try to think like an Internet user who is trying to find the information, products, and services you provide on your website. If you were an Internet user looking for your particular products, what would you type into a search engine query box? Would you be more likely to type in "beautiful art" or "framed abstract art"? Remember to concentrate on thinking like a buyer instead of a seller, and compile a list of relevant, descriptive keywords to describe the products on your website.

You can also use the Google Keyword tool, **https://support.google.com /adwords**, to find popular keywords that are relevant to your product or service and incorporate them into your headlines and content. This is also called Search Engine Optimization (SEO), the process of obtaining a high-ranking placement in search engine results. Once you have compiled your initial list of relevant keywords, you are ready to begin building the content for your website.

See Chapter 8 for ideas about adding audio and video.

One method for identifying popular styles and genres of art online is to use a keyword tool such as **www.wordtracker.com** or **www.keywordspy.com** to find out how many searches are done each month for particular types of art. For example, if you find there were 1,000 searches conducted for "landscape art" but only 50 for "abstract art," you will know that landscape art probably generates more online sales than abstract art. You can use this information to decide which types of art you should offer on your website and on online auctions like eBay.

Integrating keywords into your website content

The home page of your website should be particularly rich in keywords because it's the first page you will want visitors to find when they search for your products.

Using a particular keyword once on a webpage is not enough to obtain high search engine rankings for that page. Search engine spiders take into account not only whether a particular keyword appears on a page, but also how many times it appears in relation to the total number of words on the page. This ratio is called keyword density, and a webpage that has a high keyword density will rank better than a webpage that has a low density or a page where a keyword does not appear at all.

Internet marketers place the optimum keyword density somewhere between 1 and 4 percent for each keyword. If you construct your website content with a keyword density of 2 to 3 percent (which means that it includes every single keyword two or three times for every 100 words), you stand a good chance of having a webpage rank high in the search results for a particular keyword.

However, to keep the content readable, it is best to select one primary keyword for each webpage and one or two secondary keywords that are included at a lower keyword density.

Placement of keywords is also an important factor in obtaining high search engine rankings. Your primary keyword should appear in the first sentence of the first paragraph on the page and preferably within the first four words, if possible. It should also appear in the second paragraph and at least once in the last paragraph on the page.

Using this ratio, your website content should include a keyword at least twice for every 100 words on a webpage.

Adding readable, useful, keyword optimized content

The challenge for many website content writers is to create website copy that contains the correct density of keywords while making the content interesting and useful for the readers.

To create website content that is interesting and engaging for your readers and useful for search engine spiders, write your website content as if you were writing a letter to a friend. Use easy to read, conversational language that your visitors can relate to. Also, avoid using big or obscure words. It's tempting to use website content to showcase your vocabulary, but if your copy makes your readers reach for the dictionary too many times, they will probably lose interest and move on to another website.

Use descriptive language in your copy as well. Don't simply assume the images on your website will speak for themselves. Although well-photo-graphed, brilliant images are imperative to creating a successful art website, your readers need descriptive content to fully appreciate how incredible your artworks or crafts will look in their homes, or how energizing your music will sound when they are listening to it on the way to work or school.

Another great way to create engaging website content is through the use of stories. People love to hear stories; and if you can tell a story in your website copy, then you can be sure your visitors will more closely connect with your creative works. If you have a story behind your works, or an inspiration that you can tell a story about, it makes your website visitors more likely to want to purchase one of your works for themselves.

Using keywords in title tags

The software or web application you use for your website will require that you choose a title for each webpage. If you are using Internet Explorer, for example, this title will appear in the blue bar at the very top of the page when it is viewed online.

If you do not specify a title tag, your website creation tool will assign a generic tag to each page — Home, Page 2, Page 3, and so on. Although this may not seem like a big problem, settling on default page titles robs you of a chance to improve your page search rankings.

Instead of letting your page titles default to your website creation tool's default settings, craft your page titles around the primary keywords for each page. For example, "Abstract Art Paintings by Joe Smith" would be a good page title. You can even incorporate a secondary keyword into your page title, as long as the title is ten words or less. For example, "Abstract Art Paintings — Earthtone Paintings by Joe Smith."

Webpage description

Your website creation tool will also allow you to provide a description for each webpage. This description will not appear on the webpage itself, but it will appear in the search engine listing under the page title.

This description will give Internet users browsing search engine listings a little more information about what is contained on that page. It should be easily readable and should give your potential visitors a brief overview of what they can expect to find if they click on your link in the search engine listings.

It is also another good opportunity to use your primary and secondary keywords to improve your webpage's ranking for those keywords. Spiders will use text contained in these descriptions as a factor in determining where your webpage will rank in relation to other webpages targeting these keywords.

Image tags

Another way to improve your website's search engine ranking is to place relevant keywords in your image tags, also called ALT tags. If you have ever browsed a website and held the pointer over an image and a small yellow box appeared with a short description of the image, that's an ALT tag. Although you can look at an image and tell right away what is contained in the image, search engine spiders only know an image exists, but they cannot derive any useful information from it.

The ALT tag is a way to describe the image to the search engine spider. It is also a useful tool for loading your webpages with a few additional keywords. Your ALT tags should be short—no more than eight to ten 10 words—and should contain no more than one or two keywords. They should also accurately describe the image with words that are as specific as possible to the image's content.

Attracting visitors with faster speeds

Make sure your website operates at a fast speed. Consider speed as you choose a web host. You should also watch the size of your files. They can take too long to download if they are too large. Test each file out!

Completing a test run

Once you have finished creating your website, try searching for it through Google, Bing, or another web browser to see if it has been found and indexed by search engines. You can also use the services of a webmaster, aka, a web developer, to oversee your website and ensure that it is easily found and also operating correctly. For example, if a link on your website is not working, the webmaster can fix the issue and get you fully operational again. You can also set up a Google+ page, which allows you to link your business's Google page to your own website. Set one up easily at: **https:// plus.google.com**. You can also add links to your website on other blogs, such as when you are adding a comment on an article or post.

Cost Considerations

When you're trying to get your business off the ground, it's best to keep you budget under control. You can always upgrade or revise a website or hosting provider package at a later date. If you spend too much from the get-go, you might start off too far in the hole, which may be discouraging and hard to dig out of. Remember to keep track of your expenses.

CHAPTER 5

Creating a Blog, Enhancing Content, and Understanding Affiliated Marketing

B logging is another important tool for gaining website visibility because it exposes your website to people searching for your products via search engine and to people just looking for quality content as they surf the Internet. You can attract hundreds or thousands of visitors to your website just by writing about your art, your business, and your opinions about various aspects of your creative field.

Blogging means creating an online diary to which you add content on a regular basis. Each entry in a blog is referred to as a post, which is stamped with the date and time you submitted the entry to your blog, so that it can be posted online for the entire world to see. The posts in a blog can be arranged in chronological order (oldest to newest), reverse chronological order (newest to oldest), or by topic. Also, every blog site offers templates that you can choose from to create your look, style, and feel. Remember, this blog should look similar to your website. Consistency is key with your online presence. Use the same colors, fonts, and style throughout.

FAST FACT

In 2016, 91 percent of the galleries surveyed said they use social to help promote their gallery, artists, and artwork.[6]

There are two primary methods you can use to build a blog that will improve your website traffic. The first is to include a blog as a page, or series of pages, on your website. This will give your website visitors another reason to keep coming back to your website for new content, and it will give you yet another chance to utilize keywords to help improve your website's search engine rankings. The second is to keep a blog on one of the many popular blogging sites, such as **ghost.org**, **www.blogger.com**, **www.tumblr.com**, **www.squarespace.com**, **www.medium.com**, **www.TypePad.com**, **www.wix .com**, **www.weebly.com**, or **wordpress.com**.

---

6. Read, 2016.

You may even choose to keep more than one blog—one on your main website and one or more on other sites. This gives you the best of both worlds, because it allows you to improve your own website's content while reaching people outside of search engine queries. If you do this, it is a good idea to make sure the content on each of these blogs is at least somewhat different. Search engine spiders crawl both websites and blogs, and duplicate content may cause both to be penalized.

With over 150 million blogs on the Internet today, getting people to read your blog takes a little more than just writing about your career. There are several techniques you can use to make your blog visible, so that it can become a useful tool for your business.

Joining Blogrings

On most blogging sites, blogs are divided into categories and subcategories according to the main theme or topic of each blog. Blogrings are groups of blogs that share a common theme, interest, or predominant topic.

When you join a blogring dedicated to your particular niche in the creative arts, you will not only find other working artists with similar objectives, but you will also find their customers. An Internet user that regularly reads a blog written by a fellow artist offering similar products will also be interested in reading your blog and visiting your website to see what you have to offer.

Blogrings are also wonderful tools for networking with other working artists. By staying in contact with fellow members of an art-related blogring, you can find out about new trends in the online marketplace, contests for creative artists, new places to find discounted supplies and services, and new opportunities to get your creative works in front of the buying public and benefit from their connections. Look to join a blogring on other artists' and vendors' websites.

CASE STUDY: ZANDRA CUNNINGHAM

ZANDRA
Buffalo, NY
www.zandrabeauty.com

I started my business in 2009, I was nine years old.

I have always had a strong passion for lip balm/gloss. I would ask my dad every day before he went to work to bring me home a new lip balm. Finally, he told me NO and told me I should make my own! The rest is HISTORY!

What I like most about running my business is that I can use it as a vehicle for change. With me running my own business, I inspire others; both young and old to do the same; I love that!

Our gross profit margin is very good, and our sales are steadily increasing every year.

I operate my business inside my production studio that I have offsite. I have satisfactory equipment to currently meet the demands from our customers; however, I see a need for an upgrade to occur really soon. Both my parents and my younger brother work for me. I occasionally have my uncle and aunt work for me seasonally. Also, some of my friends will come in to help out/hang out.

For years it was very tough juggle work and school; with the last two years being the most challenging. Since the business is rising rapidly, we have decided that I will participate in homeschooling. By doing so, I can focus more on running my business while meeting the demands of school on my time, except my dad is a tough teacher!

The biggest sacrifice I have made is losing sleep. Although I don't get to hang out with my friends a lot; especially spontaneously, I really miss out on some valuable sleep.

My most satisfying moment as a business owner is being able to give back to girls' education. I really enjoy being able to help empower girls to follow their dreams

Dream BIG, Write a Plan, Follow the Plan, and Plan to have fun! I also want others to know that success comes with great sacrifice and hard work, but going through the pain, makes the success that much more gratifying.

My parents help me out a lot. Not just with helping to finance my business, but constant encouragement and motivation. The fact that my parents are proud of me helps me to deal with sacrifices. My mom is my right hand, she is my mom-a-ger and she makes sure my scheduling is on task. My dad is my CFO, he handles all of our numbers and he also is my teacher for homeschooling.

Providing Informative, Conversational Content

One of the best ways to ensure that your blog will be read is to frequently update it with content that is fresh, informative, and written in an informal, conversational style. Posting to your blog least once a week is a good rule of thumb, two to three times a week is even better. Internet users crave new content, and if you can provide relevant information that makes the reader feel more like he or she is having a conversation with a good friend and less like he or she is reading an essay, you will find that people come back to read your blog again and again.

What types of things should you blog about? You can easily use a blog to show the progress of a painting or a song you have been working on. This can be ongoing because visitors will want to check in to see how the new creative work is coming along. You can also include images or even video to show the progress of your latest creative endeavor.

So, what else can you write about? Artwork that you plan on creating soon, art shows and contests you have attended, upcoming exhibits featuring fellow artists, and even your personal life. Your blog posts should be relevant to your business, but you can also include more personal information and opinions than you do on the main pages of your website, which should focus more on your art and less on you personally.

Don't forget to include information about sales, specials (such as free shipping), or other promotions you are currently running on your website. Be sure to let them know how long your deals last so they act fast. Chapter 10 offers helpful tips on what to do if you are not a writer.

Search for similarities

You can search for websites with content relevant to yours at **www .similarsites.com**. You can also search for backlinks (links that point to your website) at: **http://www.backlinkwatch.com**.

Link building

Search engines look for certain aspects, such as key words, content, and links that appear in your website, in order to rank them on a higher level. This is called Search Engine Optimization (SEO), and, ultimately, the higher the ranking, the quicker they show up when searches are conducted by your potential customers. When it comes to links that appear in your website, the ranking considers the popularity of the link, the trustworthiness of the link, and the lack of spam that the link contains.

It's also important to make sure that your blog has the right kinds of links, popular, trustworthy, and lack of spam, to your blog. For example, you should add valuable and interesting content to your blog to make it popular and get your loyal customers to link others to your blog. The more popular your blog is, the higher it will rank in a search engine's search.

Buying links

There are a number of websites where you can purchase inbound links, or links that appear in your website that originate from another site, from quality, high-ranking websites. Many of these are link brokerages, which solicit high-ranking websites to provide links and sell the rights to these links to other website owners. These offerings are sometimes displayed and sold in an online auction format, or the website may simply have set pricing for each link.

The prices for these links can be rather steep, depending on the quality and popularity of the linking website, the fees charged by the link broker, and whether your link will appear on the website's home page or a secondary page. As an artist who is just getting their feet wet, the cost factor for inbound links may not make sense, however, it's good to know what your options are down the road when it comes to making decisions about your online presence.

Remember — your goal is to keep costs down. But if you are willing to pay for inbound links to help increase your website's search engine rankings, here are some brokerage websites that specialize in providing high-quality links: **www.linkadage.com** and **www.textlinkbrokers.com**.

Article Writing and Submission

Another way to use content to drive traffic to your website is by writing articles and submitting them to article directories, such as **www.hubpages .com**, **www.ehow.com**, and **www.examiner.com**. Signing up for a membership to an article directory is easy — just fill in your contact information and give a brief description of the types of articles you write, and you will be ready to start submitting articles for online publication and distribution. Since most article directories share a similar format, you can write your article and supporting information once via Microsoft Word or another word processing tool and quickly upload your article to multiple directories. You might also find articles to use for your own website. Make sure they are relevant to your artwork or pertain to your online presence.

You can find a list of directories at: **www.vretoolbar.com/articles/directories .php**. As noted earlier in this chapter, websites rely on content for search engine rankings, and many website owners use content taken from article directories to provide fresh copy so search engine spiders can easily find them.

The better the quality of your content, the more often website owners will use your articles for their own sites. So why would you want to write content for other people's websites? First, it establishes you as an expert in your business. By providing content to article directories that is informative and useful, you give Internet surfers the opportunity to see how much you know about your particular type of art, crafts, photography, or music.

Second, it helps your website gain exposure and traffic. When a website owner chooses to use one of your articles to build content for his or her website, he or she will be required to include your biographical information. This is a short paragraph at the end of your articles that tells the reader a little about you and provides a link to your website. Having this biographical information on another site not only provides readers with a way to see your creative works, it also helps your website gain a better search engine ranking via the one-way link included in your bio (more on link building in Chapter 10).

Third, article marketing helps to build branding on the Internet. The more articles you write and submit to article directories, the more widely known your business will become. If you write articles that resonate with readers and provide memorable information, they will remember your business the next time they need an artwork for an office, photographs for a website, or new music for a trip.

These benefits make article marketing worth your time because they will help generate more business than if you relied on search engine marketing and blogging alone.

Deciding what to write about

Articles that you write for article directories should somehow relate to your business. If you are a fine artist, your articles should relate to painting, sculpture, or whatever style of art you create. If you are a photographer, your articles should relate to some aspect of photography.

Your articles should contain practical, or "how-to," information that readers can directly apply to their own endeavors. For example, if you are a painter, your articles could be about some aspect of selecting, displaying, or creating two-dimensional artwork. Here are some examples of topics that a painter might use for articles:

- How to correctly hang and display artwork in a home or office

- How to provide optimal lighting to make artwork stand out in a room

- How to choose a painting that complements a room's style and décor

Your articles are not about selling your works, but rather about establishing yourself as a creative authority and providing information that readers can readily use in their own lives.

Submitting your article

Here are the elements required by most article directories:

- *Your Name.* This is the name that will appear as the author of the article. You can choose to use either your own name or the name of your business (e.g., Joe Smith Art Studio).

- *Your Article Category.* Most submission pages have a drop-down menu for this field, allowing you to scroll through all the available categories to choose the one that most closely fits the subject of your article.

- *Keywords.* Website owners looking for content articles can also search for keywords to find articles that will mesh well with the purpose of their sites. Choose keywords that accurately reflect the content of your article.

- *Article Summary.* This is a brief description of your article that website owners will see when they search for articles to use as content. Your article summary should be written to entice them to read the full article and use it on their websites.

  Here is an example of an article summary that will make website owners want to read your article:

  Have you ever wondered how to display a painting in your home or office so that it will perfectly complete the décor of your room? This article gives you step-by-step instructions on how to choose a location for your painting, how to select the correct height for your artwork, and how to set up your lighting so that your painting becomes an elegant conversation piece for any room.

This example description does not just tell what the article is about; it shows the reader how your article can help solve a common problem. Here's an online article summarizer that can help: **http://freesummarizer.com**.

- *Article Body.* This is the actual article you have written for publication. You should be able to simply copy and paste it from your word processor.

- *Author Bio.* Website owners that use your articles must include your biography after the article text. You can use this biography to highlight your talents and experience and provide a link to the website where you sell your creative works.

Here is an example of an author bio that will generate traffic for your website:

*Joe Smith has been creating abstract paintings for over 15 years and currently serves as the gallery design consultant for the Buckeye Art Gallery in Columbus, Ohio. To see Joe's artworks or request a commissioned painting, please visit **www.joesmithartgallery.com**.*

Affiliate Marketing

Affiliate marketing can be another good technique for driving traffic to your website and generating sales of your creative works. It involves enlisting other Internet marketers to generate interest for your website and send visitors to you.

In exchange for driving traffic to your website, affiliate marketers expect to receive a percentage of the sales that result from the traffic they send. The percentage varies according to the type of product you are selling. For physical products, such as artwork or crafts, you can offer a commission of 10 to 20 percent. For intangible products, such as digital photographic images or music downloads, you may need to offer a commission of 50 percent or more to attract affiliate marketers that will aggressively market your products.

To attract talented affiliate marketers, you may also want to offer a percentage of future sales made by repeat buyers. This percentage can be lower than the commission for the initial sale, but it will still represent an opportunity for residual commissions and will encourage your affiliates to work harder to promote your products.

Some website owners that market their products through affiliates choose to manage their own affiliate marketing programs, calculating the commissions of their affiliates and paying them via check or PayPal.

Other website owners prefer to outsource their affiliate management tasks to a third-party website, such as Commission Junction (**www.cj.com**) or ClickBank (**www.clickbank.com**). These websites list affiliate marketing opportunities and handle the calculation and payment of commissions from sales derived from affiliate marketers' efforts.

These websites also charge website owners for listing an affiliate marketing opportunity—the fee is usually less than $60 per listing. They may also charge the website owner a portion of commissions paid as compensation for calculating and managing affiliate commissions. These websites usually do not charge fees to the marketers that are promoting your products.

You can list your affiliate opportunity on Commission Junction, Click-Bank, Rakuten Marketing, and a variety of other websites. Before listing your opportunity on a website, take time to make sure that the format of the site and the types of products offered by website owners are compatible with your products—your creative works.

If you choose to offer an affiliate program to help build your online sales, it's a good idea to create a page on your website to explain your opportunity to potential affiliate marketers. You will need to explain who your target market is, tell what other kinds of marketing strategies you are using, and give your potential affiliates tips and suggestions for marketing your products. After all, you know your creative works far better than your affiliate marketers, so they will look to you for direction on how to effectively promote your works.

You should also give your affiliate marketers several advertisements that they can use in their websites, blogs, and article. (They may ask for the HTML code necessary to insert the advertisements, which you can learn more about here: **http://html.com.**) These advertisements could include graphics that link to your website and text links that point to your site.

Your advertisements should contain short messages that will entice visitors to click on the links that lead to your website. For example, you could create an advertisement with a message like, "White walls? Bring them alive with art! **www.joesmithartstudio.com.**"

You can also integrate affiliate marketing with article marketing by creating and publishing articles that encourage affiliate marketers to sign up for your program. These articles should highlight some aspect of using art to improve the décor of a home or office; or they should focus on another topic that deals with using creative works to provide enjoyment to buyers, rather than focusing on a technical aspect of art, crafting, photography, or music creation.

Although your profit percentage will be lower for creative works sold through affiliate marketers than for works sold to people who visit your website directly, you can save a significant amount of time and money by using affiliate marketing to promote your works. This is because your affiliates are responsible for promoting your products and will bear the costs of marketing.

Affiliate marketing represents an arrangement that is beneficial to both you and your affiliates. You have the opportunity to experience an increase in sales without expending additional resources for marketing, and your affiliates have the opportunity to make money through online sales without having to create their own products.

You will probably not want to depend solely on affiliates to market your products, but if you want to build your business quickly with minimal advertising costs, affiliate marketing can be an effective way to build an online fan base without spending countless hours creating marketing copy and promoting your website.

Now that you have learned about the many ways you can use online content to promote your creative works and drive traffic to your site, let us move on to another way you can improve your website's search engine rankings and attract more customers to your site via social media.

CHAPTER 6

Social Media and Discussion Boards

You likely have some kind of social media established for yourself personally, such as a Facebook or Twitter account. However, social media can also be used to promote yourself as an artist and drive visitors to your website. You can even create social media accounts specifically for your business. In this chapter, you will learn how the power of social marketing can help enhance your business while working hand in hand with your website and blog. Before we move onto social media outlets, let's briefly discuss social marketing.

What is Social Marketing?

Social marketing refers to marketing that is designed to promote the common good of a community or group, rather than to promote a product or service. If you have seen anti-tobacco commercials on television or heard them on the radio, then you have witnessed social marketing at work.

On the Internet, social marketing takes on a somewhat different meaning. When you are using social marketing online, your primary strategy is to find venues that let you benefit others through education, enlightenment, or entertainment. Your art becomes a secondary focus. The concept behind social marketing is that by building an online presence in social venues, you gain the personal interest of others, and they will naturally want to find out more about you and your art.

One way you can use social marketing to build your business is to write articles about things like the environment — a good choice if, for example, you're a photographer who concentrates on landscapes. You can also link articles and websites on your own sites and social media pages that promote causes that may fit in with your artwork or you personally.

CASE STUDY: ELISA CHONG

Owner, Sofia Anime
www.sofianime.com

My Web site is like my business card online. It helps advertise what I do. About 80 percent of my transactions are online sales.

Aside from my Web site, I use auctions, and blogs, and social networking sites to promote my business.

One of my favorite things about selling online is meeting so many new fans and collectors, and being able to chat with them. Having my art be collected all over the world. It is also a good way to advertise your art to anyone who has an Internet connection and can view the art all over the world.

One of the drawbacks of selling online is that it takes a little extra time to scan in the images, organize inventory and packing and shipping the items. It takes some of my time away from creating art.

If I had the opportunity to go back and change the way I built my online business, I would have started sooner. It is very exciting being able to meet so many collectors from all over the world, and get inspiration from them for new paintings they want to see and commission me to do.

One of the most important things you can do when building an art business online is to be very courteous to your fans and customers. Communicate well with them, offer a great product and good customer service at the same time.

Some of my best marketing methods are auctions and social networking sites, and fan groups, who help promote my art all over the Internet.

Social Media, Sharing Sites, and Messaging

Facebook

Let's start with the obvious: Facebook. Although you likely have a Facebook account to stay in touch with family and friends, it's also an excellent tool for marketing your online business.

If you don't already have an account, you can create one for free by going to **www.facebook.com** and clicking "Sign Up." Fill out your contact information, and you will be on your way to creating a profile that others can find.

With a Facebook account, you can upload personal photos and add details to your profile such as your location, your personal interests and preferences, and your website and blog addresses. You can also use your personal account to create a separate Facebook page for your business. You can find out more about this at: **www.facebook.com/help**. If you have an email account through Gmail, Facebook can also automatically notify people on your email contact list that you have a new Facebook page ready for viewing.

Having a Facebook page can be a good way for people to find you—even those you've lost touch with over the years. This includes old friends, class-mates, and colleagues, as well as previous clients who have lost your contact information.

Facebook also offers social plugins, such as the "like" button, the "share" button, embedded posts, and comments. These are tools that let you share your experiences with your Facebook friends. For example, you can "like" an art exhibit you recently visited, or you can "share" a website link. Nearly every business has a Facebook page these days, as it is the go-to place to get information and news about a company.

FAST FACT

In 2016, 57 percent of art buyers preferred Instagram while 49 percent preferred Facebook.[7]

Twitter

Twitter is fast becoming a social media choice for many, as it allows users to create and share ideas quickly and reach many users. Users post and read messages—restricted to 140 word characters—that are called "tweets." Similar to Facebook, the content on Twitter can be shared by "retweeting."

---

7. Read, 2016.

Readers can also "follow" accounts in order to read their tweets whenever they are published.

Searches can be conducted and "hashtags" (#) are used to identify messages on a specific topic — that connect Tweets on the same topic. There's also a "connect" tab that can be used to recommend accounts that may be of interest to you.

Twitter, like Facebook, is free to use. It's easy to sign up. Just go to **www .twitter.com**, click "sign up," and follow their directions. Twitter can be used to alert your readers of your new works, inspirations, upcoming art shows, sales, and more.

Instagram

Instagram is a free online mobile photo-sharing site. The site was created to allow its users to take pictures and share them either publicly or privately on the app. The pictures can also be shared through a variety of other social networking platforms, such as Facebook, Twitter, Tumblr, and Flickr (a place to show and organize photos and videos). Instagram also allows users to have a profile and a newsfeed. Like Facebook and Twitter, Instagram users can follow one another. You can sign up for Instagram at: **www.instagram .com**. You can also sign up through your Facebook account. For artists, this is a great way to share your new pieces and inspirations behind them.

FAST FACT

In 2016, 57 percent of the galleries surveyed said that Instagram was their social media platform of choice to promote their business.[8]

---

8. Read, 2016.

Pinterest

Pinterest is a free website that, like other social media platforms, requires registration to use. Pinterest users can upload, save, sort, and manage images (aka "pins") and other media content, such as videos. It is a visual bookmarking tool that is used for creative ideas. The users' personalized collections are known as pinboards. Pinterest users can browse the content of others in their feed and can also share and tweet different pinboards.

Pinterest is a great way to share inspiring images and other media to give readers a flavor of your artwork. Users can sign up through their Facebook page or by creating a new account at: **www.pinterest.com**.

Snapchat

Like Instagram, Snapchat is a mobile application that you can download to your smartphone. You can then use it to "chat" with friends through photos, videos, and captions — perhaps sending your new works of art or a picture of your latest inspiration. So, what sets Snapchat apart from the other social media outlets? After a few seconds, what you just shared is instantly deleted. Snapchat can be downloaded at: **www.snapchat.com/download**.

Flickr

Flickr is an online photo management and sharing application. Its goal is to offer new ways of organizing photos and videos, as well as to help people make their content available to their audience. The Flickr community is currently home to 13 billion photos, 120 million people, and 2 million groups. Users can check what is trending, view recent photos and galleries and more.

For those who are photo savvy or who are working to promote their photographs, Flickr makes sense as a place to show their works or to get inspired. To join, you sign up with a Yahoo email account. Your email address is requested on the sign-up form, as is some personal information, such as your name. A code is sent to your email and then you're good to go. Sign up at: **https://login.yahoo.com/account/create**.

Instant Messengers

Kik is a free instant messenger software application for mobile devices for use on iOS, Android, and Windows Phone operating systems. A data plan or a WiFi must be connected in order to use Kik. Individuals or groups can be messaged at the same time, and an unlimited number of messages can be received by anyone else who has a Kik account.

Many people use Kik as an alternative to emailing or public chatting on other social networking sites. It is one of the most popular chat platforms available. When using Kik, an artist can send updates on their works, reminders of upcoming art shows, and more. Kik can be downloaded at: **www.kik.com**.

Another similar app is Whatsapp, which can be downloaded at: **www.whatsapp.com**.

Bot shops

Kik has recently added a Bot Shop where their users can chat with companies. For example, a health and beauty company like Sephora can interact directly with users via text and chat.

Other companies, and even one-person enterprises, are also jumping in to create their own Bot Shop. Even Facebook is working on a similar tool. This goes to show that direct and personalized information and exchange is the way to go when trying to acquire and keep new business. To build a bot, visit: **https://dev.kik.com/#/home**.

LinkedIn

With over 400 million members, LinkedIn is the world's largest professional networking site. Joining allows you to build your identity, find new business opportunities, and stay in touch with other professionals, colleagues, and classmates. On LinkedIn, you can upload your résumé, information about your business, and much more. And it's free and easy to join. Find out more at: **www.linkedin.com.**

Discussion Boards

Another good way to use social marketing to build your business is by participating in discussion boards. Discussion boards are where Internet users can have asynchronous conversations that may last hours, days, or even months. The discussion is moved forward when each person posts a message relating to the previous message, or to the topic that is being discussed. Groups of related posts are organized in threads, which show the chronology of the discussion from the beginning post that initiated the discussion to the most recent post. Discussion board threads continue until the original topic has been thoroughly discussed, or until the participants tire of the discussion and move on to another topic.

A discussion board may have threads on several topics at once—larger discussion boards with many active participants may have hundreds of active threads being updated with new posts.

Most discussion boards follow a general theme or interest. There are discussion boards for people to discuss a wide range of interests, from art, to music, to food, to nearly any other interest or general topic you could imagine. This allows people with common interests to gather for networking, idea sharing, or just idle chatter.

You can find message boards in a couple of different ways. First, you can use a message board directory to find boards related to your particular interest. There are numerous message board directories that list thousands of boards to choose from. One of these directories is **www.boardhost.com**, which lists discussion boards categorized according to a number of general topics.

Another good discussion board directory is Google Groups, available at: **https://groups.google.com/forum/#!overview**. This website contains links to hundreds of message boards on a wide variety of topics. You can find discussion boards focused on fine arts, crafts, music, and photography. Another similar directory is Yahoo! Groups: **https://groups.yahoo .com/neo**.

Many discussion boards are part of websites that owners use to increase traffic to their sites so they can promote their products and services to discussion board members.

The discussion board at **www.wetcanvas.com** is one example of an art-related board that is part of a larger website. The website home page provides links to articles about various topics of interest to artists as well as links to contests that creative people can enter to gain exposure and win cash prizes. The discussion board that is part of this website has hundreds of members and contains discussions on topics such as art techniques, what kinds of materials artists use, and how they sell their art online. It also contains a number of topics only loosely related to art (and some not related to art at all), so members can have general discussions about random topics while they are taking a break from their creative works.

The WetCanvas message board is a particularly useful tool for artists and other creative people because its members tend to be serious about promoting art online and about helping fellow creative people to reach success on the Internet.

Another popular discussion board is available at **www.ebsqart.com**. You may register on this discussion board either as a patron or as an artist. To register as an artist, you will need to become a member of EBSQ (you can apply for a membership by visiting the membership link on the website's home page). On the EBSQ discussion board, you will find many artists who are serious about establishing a profitable business online and many patrons who are interested in supporting and promoting the careers of working artists.

If you sell a portion of your creative works on eBay, or you are considering it, another great resource is the collection of discussion boards available on

www.ebay.com. There are several art-related discussion boards and even a board just for artists that allows people like you to discuss the ins and outs of selling creative works on eBay. This can be a valuable resource for you, because you can learn from the trials and the mistakes that other artists have made when building their own art businesses.

Promoting your works through discussion boards

As with any type of social marketing, the key to successful marketing on discussion boards lies in taking a somewhat passive approach, rather than putting your business front and center. You will want to build online relationships through your discussion board postings, rather than just showing up and promoting your art to a group of people who do not know you.

When you find a discussion board that matches your interests, the first thing you should do after you register is to look for a "new members" section. This section will typically contain threads that will give you information on the board's terms of use — what you may and may not post on the discussion board, and in which sections you can post certain types of content. It is important to read through these threads before you submit your first post to the discussion board.

Respecting a discussion board's terms of use and general rules of etiquette will go a long way toward helping you establishing online relationships that can advance your creative career.

After you have read through the terms of use and general etiquette threads, you are ready to begin posting messages on the discussion board. You will want to start with the board's "Introduce Yourself" thread. This is a good place to give members information about your background, your interests, and general information about the types of art you like to create.

Introduction threads are also good places to start building relationships with members of the board, so make sure your introductory post is colorful and interesting. Tell members things about your life, such as what medium you work in, what city and state you live in, what your hobbies are, and what your plans are for your artwork. A short introduction will help you get many responses from members who are welcoming you to the board.

After you have submitted an introductory post, get involved in some of the other discussions currently developing on the board. Let other members know you are reading their posts by replying with posts that comment on their insights, ask for elaboration, or otherwise reference their posts. People like to talk about themselves and will feel more connected to you if they know you are interested in their opinions and insights.

Over time, you will develop close relationships with some of the other board members, and you will find these members will be more than willing to help you promote your business by letting friends, family, and business associates know about your art. No artist can create works that everyone will like and appreciate, so when other board members find a potential client who is looking for a style or type of creative work that they do not provide, they will be glad to refer those people to you.

Likewise, if you create abstract paintings, and you meet a potential client who is looking for bronze sculpture, do not hesitate to refer that person to a discussion board member that creates art from bronze. Helping out other creative business owners will go a long way toward establishing relationships with them, so they will be more inclined to send you business as well.

Here is one point to keep in mind when you are writing discussion board posts — some discussion boards do not allow members to link to their websites in posts. This keeps people from joining boards for the sole purpose of posting advertisements.

However, some discussion boards may have sections or subsections where this rule does not apply. If this is the case, these sections will be clearly marked and may contain terms of use or rules of etiquette that are separate from those governing the rest of the board. You can use these sections to advertise your website, your blog, or any other marketing site or page you have built to promote your creative works. Just make sure that you read the discussion board rules and that you follow them.

Using your profile and personal signature to drive traffic

If a discussion board doesn't allow members to specifically talk about your business, you may wonder how users will be able to find your website. There are two primary ways of accomplishing this. One is by providing your website link in your personal profile, and the other is by linking to your website in your signature.

When you register on a discussion board, you will have the opportunity to build a personal profile. This may include a photograph or image, your name, your location, your blog and website addresses, and other information you choose to provide.

As you build relationships on discussion boards, other members who read your posts will visit your profile to learn more about you. From there, they can click the links to visit your website, blog, or other promotional pages.

You will also have the opportunity to write a custom signature, which will appear beneath each of your discussion board posts. Most discussion boards allow website links in signatures, so you can include your website address here so that people reading your posts can immediately visit your site or blog.

When writing your signature, make sure to review the site's terms of use to find out how many links you can include—some discussion boards limit you to two or three links. If you have more than three blogs or websites, provide links to your most effective ones and make sure that these sites also link to all your others.

Now that you have learned how to use social marketing to further expand your online reach, let's move on to another way you can promote and sell your works — via eBay, ArtFire, Amazon, and Spreesy.

CHAPTER 7

Selling Your Products Through Etsy, Artfire, Handmade at Amazon, and Spreesy

In addition to driving your customers to your website, enticing them with your blog, meeting them through discussion boards, and connecting with them through your numerous  social media platforms (such as Facebook, Twitter, and Pinterest), there are other Internet spots where you can create a virtual marketplace.

The Internet is now a vibrant marketplace for artists seeking to promote and sell their works of fine art. A decade ago, few people would have believed that artists could create financially successful business without contracting with a physical gallery. However, in today's world, the Internet is vastly used for banking, schooling, socializing, and purchasing. Furthermore, although it used to be that artists showed their works in galleries alone, today, there are thousands of artists who have built successful businesses online without having ever displayed an artwork in a physical gallery. The same goes for musicians and photographers. Nearly everything is being sold online these days. Artwork of any type has become a valuable addition to the Internet, because users can browse and select pieces without the hassle of visiting a gallery, dealing with salespeople, and paying marked up prices for original fine art.

The Internet has also leveled the field for artists by giving them the ability to control the display, marketing, and prices of their own creative works. They no longer have to rely on gallery owners to tell them what their artwork is worth, or pay large commissions to galleries for the privilege of displaying their art. Artists are now able to control the business aspects of selling art and can build lucrative businesses with their own creativity and marketing efforts.

Like any business, selling art online takes a quite a bit of perseverance and ingenuity, along with a little luck. This chapter will give you some things to consider while you are building your business, promoting your art, and pursuing even more online avenues to sell your creations.

Using Your Art to Create Your Online Identity

When you are choosing artwork to sell online, it is important to remember that every piece of art you display will become part of your online identity. Buyers will come to know you not only for your blog posts and articles but also for the type of artwork you sell online.

For this reason, it is crucial that your online portfolio conveys a sense of continuity and consistency, as we discussed in Chapter 2. Many online artists want to sell works that reflect a variety of genres and styles — either because they want visitors to see that they are versatile or because they simply want to experiment with different types of art.

While experimentation is crucial for an artist to continue to evolve, it is much easier to build a successful business if the artwork you display online shares a similar connection. This is not to say that all your artwork needs to look virtually the same, but it should share some common traits. For example, you may use architectural elements as a common element of the works you place for sale. Your style may vary somewhat throughout your online portfolio, but the common theme of architectural elements should carry through all of your fine art.

Although it demonstrates versatility, displaying many different types of artwork on the same website without a common thread tends to confuse visitors. When viewing your works, visitors may have difficulty understanding your artistic vision, and it could become impossible for them to associate a particular style of art with your name.

Create continuity throughout your online galleries, and you will find it much easier to build a loyal customer base that will return to your website to purchase art from you time and time again. Remember that it is important to keep this in mind for all of your online stores and online sites, such as your website, your Twitter page, and your Pinterest account. Your presence needs to have consistency in all that you put forth.

So, let's get started and look at a few ideas for online stores, including Etsy, Artfire, Handmade at Amazon, and Spreesy, which is actually a tool designed to help you sell more through your various online platforms.

Etsy

Etsy is an online marketplace of vintage and handmade goods, such as jewelry, tie-dye clothing, crafts, games, paintings, books, and more. There are more than one million sellers on Etsy, which is a good thing because buyers have a wide selection of items to look at. However, the bad thing is that there are so many choices out there that it is sometimes hard to stand out from the crowd. This is again where

consistency in your look, style, and feel are important, as is always putting your best foot forward.

FAST FACT

Etsy first began after a woodworker had a difficult time selling a wood-encased computer. He joined with some friends to create Etsy to help crafters easily sell their work.[9]

CASE STUDY: MOZIAH "MO" BRIDGES

14-Year-Old Fashion Designer and
   Entrepreneur
Founder of Mo's Bows and Shark Tank
   Contestant

Mo's Story

I started my company when I was nine years old, and I started because I couldn't find any other bowties that really fit my style or my personality. So, that's when I asked my grandmother to teach me how to sew. From that point, I started an Etsy, and then, I would sell my bowties for bags of chips or trade them for rocks. We would go out to farmer's markets, and we would do local shows and local trunk shows. After that, I would make it into the newspaper, and then the newspaper contacted the magazine. And then the magazine went to the show, and then the show went from show to show to show to show. I didn't think it would get this big, but my hard work and dedication led me to this point.

Shark Tank actually called us and they wanted us to be on the show. Originally, my mom said no because she didn't want to have us crying on the show. We went out to LA, and we shot the show, but it wasn't for sure that we were actually going be on the show; it was just, like, a thing that we did. But then, when it got to that point, we were so excited that we got the opportunity.

---

9. Zacks Research Staff, 2015.

If you didn't see the show, I didn't walk away with the check, but Daymond [John] did offer to be my mentor. He's just been guiding me through the practical aspects of owning my own company. He's taught me always to stay true to your company and never sell out your brand. Always know your brand, and just be yourself. My particular brand is fashionable with a touch of class, and urban.

[Mo's Bows bowties] are in a lot of stores. I have 12 to 15 stores that they're in right now, but, where I get most of the profit is from online, and that's my website at **mosbowsmemphis.com.** Someone helped me [make the website]. We have a whole Mo's Bows team that helps.

Advice for Teens Interested in Fashion

I would tell them to always figure out what you like doing and find out how you can make a profit out of it. And, also, just to be true to yourself and believe in yourself. I think believing in yourself means invest in yourself, and just stay true to your brand, like Daymond always taught me.

I do give back to the community. I have my Go Mo! Summer Camp Scholarship, and 100 percent of the proceeds help kids go to summer camp, because in Memphis it's hot, and childhood hunger is at its highest in the summertime because kids aren't eating that nutritious meal [that they're eating] when school time is in. So, I figured they can have fun, go to the movies, go to the swimming pool, and just be kids.

Future Goals

I want to be a fashion designer, and I want to have my own clothing line by the time I'm 20. I want to go to Parsons School of Design and hopefully get a Range Rover in the process of that.

Setting up your shop

The first thing you want to do to get onto Etsy is to go to **www.etsy.com** and familiarize yourself with their Seller Handbook. It's located under "Sell on Etsy," and it contains a wealth of important information, such as how to produce the best photographs of your products, how to develop and promote your brand to shoppers, and to how to incorporate growth strategies so your business keeps booming. You can also subscribe to Etsy's newsletter, "Etsy Success." This newsletter is delivered to your email address and offers articles, tips, and seller resources.

If you want to connect with other sellers around the world, Etsy has an online community that you can join where you can connect. You can also join a community discussion group, contact the Etsy Help Center, or watch an online webinar and learn some of the "how to's" by watching an online video presentation.

Another cool thing about Etsy is that you can become an affiliate and earn commission. (We discussed affiliate marketing in Chapter 5.) Once you have familiarized yourself with the online offerings, you might just be ready to set up your own shop. Just click on "Sell on Etsy" at the top of the home page, and you can choose your shop name and begin creating listings. You will also decide on what payment methods you will accept and add your billing information. You will also add your shop policies, configure your shipping options, set up shipping profiles, and create an "About" section for your shop. Additionally, you will create a look by uploading a shop icon and a cover photo. Although this may all seem daunting, it's relatively easy, thanks to Etsy's step-by-step process and their easy-to-follow Seller's Handbook. Remember you can also call their Help Center if you have questions or need further assistance.

FAST FACT

Employees at Etsy go to "Etsy School" where they learn about a variety of subjects like Mindfulness 101 and Feminism and Technology.[10]

---

10.   Zacks Research Staff, 2015.

Working your shop

As mentioned, there are a lot of people shopping on Etsy, and there are also a lot of people looking to sell. The best thing you can do it put your best foot forward. Sign up for the newsletter, review the Seller's Handbook until you know the tips and tricks that are used by the best sellers on Etsy, read the online articles, such as How to Promote your Stuff on Social Media, join the online communities and discussion groups, and participate in an Online Lab where you can watch live or archived Etsy Webinars. Also, don't forget to mention on your blog, website, and Twitter page that you have an online shop at Etsy.

Paying your fees

There are a few fees associated with selling on Etsy. There are no monthly fees. However, there are listing fees ($.20 per listing) and a fee that is $3.5% of the selling price (not including shipping costs or tax rates you might charge). There are also fees for processing credit or debit cards, Etsy gift cards, Apple Pay, integrated PayPal, iDEAL (Netherlands), and Sofort (Austria and Germany) payments. A complete breakdown of all fees, all of which are reasonable, are available at **www.etsy.com/help/article/136**.

Keeping track of your shop

The best way to keep track of your Etsy shop is to track your expenses, your time, and your goods. You can use a notebook, and there are also small business journals that you can find at an office supply store that include ledgers for inventory, sales, cash on hand, and more. Etsy also has an expense tracking template that you can find here: **https://www.etsy.com/seller-handbook/article/tips-for-tracking-your-business-expenses/26593272798**.

FAST FACT

Etsy stock rose 86% from 2016 to 2017.[11]

It's important to keep track of every part of your business so you know how much money you are spending, what is selling well and what is not, and how much money you are earning. This is also important for your tax considerations, which we discussed in Chapter 2 and will discuss more of in Chapter 11.

ArtFire

Another online option that you should consider is ArtFire. Like Etsy, it's a place to sell handmade and vintages goods as well as crafting supplies.

---

11.   Borchardt, 2017.

Setting up your shop

To set up a shop with ArtFire, register at **artfire.com**. There, you will enter your name, username, email address, and password. Try to keep this information consistent with your other online sites, such as Twitter and your website. Once your account is created, you will need images for your shop banner and avatar. You will also create a short bio of yourself or your work, create a welcome message, and arrange your shop sections—for example, "Drawings and Paintings." You can also choose your payment options, and you can link your social media pages to your ArtFire shop. All of this is thoroughly explained on their ArtFire Help Center section at **www.artfire .com/modules.php?name=help_center&op=details&id=70**.

Working your shop

If you have questions or need advice, you can join ArtFire's online community forums and interact with other sellers. You can also review ArtFire's blog at **www.artfire.com/blog**, where you can find advice for sellers, read about tips for your own shop, gain inspiration, sign up for weekly emails, and more. There's also an excellent Help Center.

Paying your fees

ArtFire offers a choice of plans that range from a Standard Shop to a Popular Shop to a Featured Shop. The fees and features of each account differ, so you can choose the best one for your business. For example, the Popular Shop is $20 for up to 1,000 listings, with a 3 percent final valuation fee and no contract. The Featured Shop is $40 and offers up to 2500 listings with a 3 percent final valuation fee and no contract. What you are selling, how much you have to sell, and how much time and effort you can put into your online shop will help determine what plan makes the most sense for you. A complete list of plans and what they offer is available at **www.artfire .com/ext/sell/starttoday**.

Keeping track of your shop

The best way to keep track of your online shop at ArtFire is to track your expenses, your time, and your goods. You can use notebooks or small business journals that you can find at an office supply store. It's important to keep track of every part of your business so you know how much money you are spending, what is selling and what is not, and how much money you are earning. You can also use a software accounting system like Quicken, which retails for a price starting at $39.99. Keeping track of your business is also important for your tax considerations.

Handmade at Amazon

Handmade at Amazon is a newer store at **www.amazon.com** that was created to allow artists, like yourself, the chance to reach millions of customers online. The beauty of Amazon's name is that almost everyone has heard of it, has shopped on it, and has good things to say about their experience, as it is a well-established company with a solid background.

Setting up your shop

To set up a Shop at Handmade at Amazon, you will first register with your name and email address and then receive a link to get the process started. You will then create a profile and receive a custom URL for your business. After this, you can list your products and start to sell. Listings are free and do not expire. The products must be handmade, not made from a kit. Other sellers on Handmade at Amazon include those who are making and selling baby items, stationary, artwork, toys, games, and more. You can also choose to sell at Handmade at Amazon along with another online shop like Etsy. You can have more than one online shop if you choose, but it may be wise to select just a few, since you have to keep track of every shop, blog, and website you have. Too many can be too much.

Working your shop

When you create your profile page, you are encouraged to be creative (remember to be consistent with your other online presence, such as your website). You can also set up pages for each of your products so you can describe them well. You can also add imagery to go with each product. You will decide on shipping options, payments, promotions, and more. Amazon also offers a Help Center that you can call or email should you need assistance or have questions, which you can find here: **www.amazon.com /gp/help/customer/display.html/ref=asus_hnd_lp_fees?nodeId =201818920&ld=NSGoogle**.

Paying your fees

Currently, Handmade at Amazon has a 15 percent referral fee that includes payment processing, marketing, discounted shipping, and fraud protection. They have waived their monthly fee at this time. You can find the complete list of fees as well as more information at **www.amazon.com/gp/help /customer/display.html/ref=asus_hnd_lp_fees?nodeId=201818920&ld =NSGoogle**.

Keeping track of your shop

Like their regular site, Handmade at Amazon has an online tracking system that will help you keep track of inventory and sales. There's also a way to pay for and print shipping labels.

Another way to keep track of your online shop at Handmade at Amazon is to track your expenses, your time, and your goods. You can use notebooks or small business journals, which you can find at an office supply store. It's important to keep track of every part of your business so you know how much money you are spending, what is selling and what is not, and how much money you are earning. As mentioned before, this is also extremely important for your tax considerations.

Spreesy

If you are a musician looking to sell an album or an MP3, or an author who is looking to sell an e-book, then Spreesy might be the way to go. Spreesy is a social commerce solution that lets you list products and sell them wherever your online customers are located — such as your Instagram, Facebook, and Pinterest accounts. With Spreesy, your social media sites become selling tools to promote your physical and digital products. Plus, you can integrate your Spreesy shop with your other shops like Etsy. And it's free to join.

Setting up your shop

Once you have created an account, you can use a mobile app to tap into it.

You will first create an account with your email and a password. Once you have an account, you will press the "post" button on your products dashboards. You can then select which networks you'd like to post to, customize your post caption, and post your product for sale.

Working your shop

Spreesy currently supports selling through your Instagram, Facebook, Twitter, Pinterest, Spreesy stores, and email. However, there are likely new additions right around the corner as the social media world keeps growing.

Paying your fees

Spreesy charges a flat 3 percent transaction fee on a per transaction basis. They don't charge listing fees or monthly fees, and there are no hidden fees. Your payments are sent to your own PayPal account. Find out more about PayPal at **www.paypal.com**. You can open an account there for free. We will discuss more about receiving payments in Chapter 11.

Keeping track of your shop

On Spreesy, you will have a dashboard that helps keep track of some of your information, such as prices and quantities. However, it's also a good idea to keep track of your expenses, your time, and your goods. As mentioned earlier, you can use a notebook or small business journals that you can pick up at an office supply store. It's important to keep track of every part of your business so you know how much money you are spending, what is selling and what is not, and how much money you are earning. This information will come in handy when tax season rolls around, which we discussed in Chapter 2 and will discuss more of in Chapter 11.

By no means has this chapter touched on every online option available. There are lots of others out there that may work for your business, and even more arrive on the scene every year. In Chapter 9, we will learn how to sell on eBay and Artsy, to a smaller degree, which are where online auctions are hosted. Also, in Chapter 8, we will discuss other options for online sales. Yes, there are plenty more options to sell your work online!

CHAPTER 8

Where Else Can You Sell Online?

While you may consider selling your arts and crafts at flea markets, craft malls, art festivals, and other local events, there are still more online places that you can try to sell your wares. Handmade toys, decorations, quilts, clay figurines, dolls, mosaics, photographs, paintings, prints, and more can all be successfully sold on the Internet through locations other than your website, Etsy, Handmade at Amazon, and Spreesy.

Although this book focuses on selling online, viable options may also include the previously-mentioned places like your local flea market or art festival. When setting up a booth, you can include business cards that included with your online store information, such as the title of your store and the URL. Yes, the possibilities are endless with Internet sales, and during this chapter, we will look at even more options out there. Finding the right location to sell your artwork takes some time and effort, however. It's best to choose a few locations that you feel might work best and go with those. Don't forget to ask around, read reviews, and see what other artisans, craftspersons, and musicians have said about the place you are considering.

Creative Sites and Classifieds

Artwork, images, and photographs

Below is a list of places that might work best for paintings, drawings, crafts, and other creations. Also provided is a short summary for each, along with contact information. For information about photographing your image correctly, see Chapter 9.

ArtPal

Art Pal has over 75,000 artists who are selling original art, prints, and custom framing. It's free to list up to 30 pieces of artwork on ArtPal, and you get to keep 95 to 100 percent of the profits. The payments are processed by ArtPal, and the funds are posted to your chosen account directly. You can sell and ship on your own, or you can have ArtPal take care of it. You can also create an account where you can list up to 7,000 items for only $29 a year. Starting your own gallery takes only minutes. Remember, you should also share your ArtPal gallery with your social media sites, such as Facebook and Twitter. Find out more at **www.artpal.com**.

Artplode

Artplode is an online art gallery where dealers, artists, and galleries buy and sell art with no commission charged to either parties. Artplode only charges when an item sells, and they do not charge for listing. The fees are $60 per piece of artwork that is advertised. Once it is sold, there is no additional charge to you or the buyer. To register, all you have to do is register your email, and create a password. Once you have an account created, you can choose how many pieces you want to list. You should also share your Artplode gallery with your social media sites, such as Facebook and Twitter. Find out more at **www.artplode.com**.

Fine Art America

With over 10 million images for sale, Fine Art America is the world's largest art marketplace and print-on-demand technology company. The images you sell are purchased as framed prints, greeting cards, and more. In addition, the site offers tools to help artists with sales and marketing, such as setting up branded web stores and selling prints on Facebook. It's easy to create an account, list your products, set your prices, and begin selling. There are a variety of membership plans with a variety of benefits, like the standard plan (which is free) and the premium plan. The profit depends on the mark up that you decide for the image. Fine Art America sets a standard for sizes and mediums, and you earn what you can get above that standard. Find out more at **www.fineartmaerica.com**.

Imagekind

Another fast-growing art community can be found at **www.imagekind. com.** Imagekind focuses on selling and producing your work with the highest quality framed giclée prints and great attention to detail. You can enjoy unlimited uploads, get a dedicated URL that you can use on your social media sites, display your work to a wide audience, and retain the copyright of your work. You keep 100 percent of the profit of the markup that you set from their base price, and you can earn additional dollars on frames, mats, and glazing. There are several accounts to choose from, such as the platinum and the pro, that offer a variety of benefits. Find out more at **www.imagekind.com/sell/art-photography.aspx**.

Foap

If you have a smartphone, you can download Foap's free app and start selling your photographs. For each photo you sell, you earn $5. Plus, you can sell the same photo an unlimited number of times. Find out more at **www.foap.com**.

Music

iTunes

iTunes requires that you complete an application. Signing up is free. A Tax ID is required upon sign up. Additional sales terms are available upon sign up. Books and movies can also be sold on iTunes. Your content becomes available on iTunes Radio. Tracks are typically .99 each; albums are $9.99. You earn a play per pay fee when played on iTunes Radio. Sales are tracked online. For details and information, visit **www.apple.com/itunes/working -itunes/sell-content/music-faq.html**.

Audio and video

YouTube

YouTube might be something to consider if you want to make your own videos and send viewers to your website or online store. For example, you could video yourself painting a picture or composing a song. You can also reference that you are on YouTube on your social media sites and provide the link to your work on YouTube. Signing up is easy. Find out more at **www.youtube.com**.

Podcasts

A podcast is a digital audio presentation that you can create and add to your blog or other sites. You can create interesting messages and even develop a series and have your readers subscribe to your podcast. For a podcast, you will need a microphone, a computer or smartphone, and recording software such as Garageband ($4.99 in the Apple store) or Audacity (free software).

Once you have your recording equipment set up, you can then create a podcast or short audio file on a topic that applies to the arts. Once you have completed your recording, you can upload your podcast to your blog. Alert your readers via email and your social media outlets that it has posted. Audacity offers a step-by-step explanation of how to publish a podcast and generate a Rich Site Summary (RSS) feed at **http://wiki.audacityteam .org/wiki/How_to_publish_a_Podcast**.

What is RSS? RSS allows for a wide audience to see and reach your content. Your audience can subscribe to a variety of RSS feeds that can be found on websites or blogs with feeds. RSS subscribers download feed readers, such as Feedly, that help organize content on the web, such as the latest news or trends. Find out more at **www.feedly.com**.

Patreon

Patreon allows your fans to help fund your ongoing project through a monthly subscription of their choice. You create what you want to share with your fans, such as a "how-to" video on painting a landscape, and they help fund your artwork by subscribing to the special stuff that you post for them. This helps bring in the money to buy more supplies, offers you times to concentrate on your artwork, and helps pay the bills, such as your financing your website. Signing up is free and easy. Patreon charges payment fees (5 percent when your patrons add to your balance) and payout fees ($0.25 per payout to 2 percent of 1-20, depending on the type of account, such as your bank or PayPal account) only when you move your funds to your bank. Find our more at **www.patreon.com**.

Other places to consider

There are many other places you can look to get your name out there and sell more artwork online. Below are a few words about each. Check them out and see if they could work for you.

CafePress

At CafePress, you upload a design and they sell the design on products, such as t-shirts and coffee cups. Once you upload an image, CafePress suggests what types of products the image would work best with, such as on a mousepad or calendar. Then they market your image, printed on the products, and you profit. There are no upfront costs. Profits vary depending on the item. Find out more at **www.cafepress.ca**.

Craigslist

Craigslist offers a wide range of products that some are looking to buy and some are looking to sell. Some items are used and some are new. It's a classified ad forum where arts and crafts is one of the categories where your art might be sold. It's free to list. You list the items, and the purchase is made at an agreed time and place. Find out more at **www.craigslist.org**. But before you go, be sure to read the next section, "What to Watch Out for When Selling Online."

OfferUp

OfferUp works in a similar fashion as Craigslist, except it focuses solely on buyers and sellers. It works via app, and listings can be found easily and sold quickly. Users have profiles, buyers and sellers have ratings, and contacts are made in real time. It's free to list. You list the items and the purchase is made at an agreed upon time and place. Find out more at **www .offerupnow.com**. But before you go, be sure to read the next section, "What to Watch Out for When Selling Online."

VarageSale

VarageSale allows local community members in over 300 communities to buy and sell in a variety of categories — such as clothing, tools, furniture, and even arts and crafts. Items are posted for sale, and messages are sent to arrange for a time and place to meet and complete the transaction. VarageSale sometimes has big events where a large VarageSale is held in one location with plenty of buyers and sellers. "Praises" can be left for the seller if the buyers are happy once the transaction is complete. It's free to list on varagesale.com and is available on some mobile devices. Find out more at **www.varagesale.com**. But before you go, be sure to read the next section, "What to Watch Out for When Selling Online."

What to Watch Out for When Selling Online

Keeping track of sales

Even though you may have an online sales tracker with your inventory, you still want to keep an outside record of your sales to help ensure accuracy. A simple notebook will work, and any office supply store has record-keeping journals that have pages for sales, inventory, expenses, and more. There are also software programs, like Quicken, that you can purchase for about $39.99 for a Starter Edition. Find out more about Quicken at **www. quicken.com**. We will discuss more about finances and how to keep track in Chapter 11.

Ensuring your payment

Again, don't assume the site you are selling on has an up-to-date list of your sales and payments. Some may, and some may not. It all depends on the plan you sign up for and the companies, like Etsy or ArtFire, that you have signed up with. Your best bet for record accuracy is to always keep track of records as well in a notebook or ledger. Make sure that you read the fine print about how you will get paid, when you will get paid, and how much you will receive after any cut is taken by the. Always call the company's Help Center if you have any questions. It's important to be clear when it comes to money.

Staying safe with online sales connections

Some websites, forums, and communities are good options to try to sell your work. But again, it's important to be clear about how and when you will get paid. A classified ad site, like Craigslist or OfferUp, offers a chance to list your goods to your local community. It's best in circumstances like these to keep safety in mind. Try to meet the person in the parking lot of your local precinct or at a local restaurant with security cameras if you are making a cash sale to sell one of your pieces. Don't take a check or money order. Take cash only. Bring someone with you like a parent or guardian. Don't go alone.

Reading the reviews

Remember to check out what others are saying about a website, forum, or online store before signing up. It's best to hear the inside story from someone who has purchased goods or sold goods at the places you are considering. Make a note of it. If there have been a lot of unhappy customers, then don't waste your time trying to sell there. If your customers aren't happy with their purchasing experience, they will be less happy with your artwork.

FAST FACT

In 2016, 65 percent of buyers said that the customer reviews and feedbacks were an important factor in the buying process.[12]

---

12. Read, 2016.

Photographing your artwork

Your images must be clear, properly lit, and free of visual distortions so your buyers can closely approximate what your artworks will look like in their homes and offices. And, generally speaking, more is better when it comes to photos. Shooting the artwork from several angles and distances helps the buyer "see" your art's details, dimensions, and overall feel.

It is a good idea to set up a "staging" area where you can photograph all your paintings or sculptures for your auctions. By doing this, you can arrange your lighting and your tripod position a single time, which will provide consistent results and save you a great deal of time.

Ideally, the background on which you place your artworks should be flat black. This will reduce the amount of color distortion appearing in your photos. You can accomplish this either by painting a wall black or by stretching black fabric over a portion of a wall.

When it comes to lighting, you should use soft white light sources set at 45-degree angles on either side of the painting. The light source on one side of the painting should be slightly closer to the painting than the light source on the other side. This will help eliminate glare and harsh shadows that can ruin the look of your photos.

If your camera has it, use the "optical zoom" feature to take close-up shots of your paintings. Some digital cameras are only equipped with "digital zoom," which is fine for taking pictures of the new family car for Grandma, but not so good for capturing fine details of your art. If digital zoom is all you have available, it's better to skip the close-up shots altogether.

And always use a tripod. It is surprising how many artists have every other element covered for creating good photographs, and then the pictures come out blurred because they were not willing to spend $20 on a serviceable tripod. A good tripod can make all the difference between clear, professional looking images and sloppy, fuzzy pictures.

One last thought on photos. If you browse through eBay art auctions, you will notice that quite a few artists have photos of their artwork in rooms that look like they came out of a furniture catalogue. In the majority of cases, the "rooms" are indeed images lifted from other websites. The artworks are then cropped out of other photos and superimposed in the room. Supposedly, this gives the buyer a better idea of how an artwork will look in a living space.

It is not clear if "staging" your artworks in this way helps your sales at all. Some successful eBay artists use this technique in every auction, others do not use it at all, and there are a number of artists who feel that the technique is an unfair and unethical representation of a piece of art.

The only advice that can be given here is that if you feel you need to do this, try to refrain from using images from other websites. It is not uncommon for artists to run into copyright infringement issues as a result of using images without permission. Of course, if you are like most of us, you do not have a room that is straight out of IKEA (stage lighting and all), so it may be difficult to create the sort of pristine environment for your artwork without using a stock image.

One more piece of advice: Check with the individual sites that you are uploading to find out the size expectations of your images. You want to make sure your images are the right size so they upload correctly.

Now that we have covered more online options and how to photograph your work, let's talk about ways that you can sell your good via online auctions, such as eBay and Artsy.

CHAPTER 9

Participating in Online Auctions

In this section, you will learn about using online auctions on eBay and Artsy to generate additional sales, as well as increase traffic to your website and other online accounts.

eBay

People who visit eBay are generally looking for a bargain. However, when it comes to original artwork, there is a large pool of buyers who are looking to purchase art at reasonable prices.

eBay serves as an excellent resource for working artists, crafters, musicians, and photographers. Hundreds of creative people earn a comfortable living from eBay sales alone, and thousands more use eBay auctions to augment their gallery and other online sales.

FAST FACT

eBay first launched in September 1995. The first item sold on the site was a broken laser pointer.[13]

This website receives hundreds of thousands of visitors each day. When you post a featured auction listing to sell one of your artworks on eBay, it is not uncommon for your auction to receive 200 or more visits in a week.

CASE STUDY: DIANE DOBSON-BARTON

Owner, Artist How-To
(620) 473-2166
www.artist-how-to.com

I began listing art on eBay in about 1996. I then created a basic website that has grown over the years. Today, online sales are at least 80-90% of my total sales.

I use eBay, ETSY, blogs (Wordpress, Blogger, Live Journal), and networking sites (MySpace, Facebook, Indiepublic) to promote my online art business. However, my Web site is also a crucial element of my marketing efforts – it is vital to all of my business transactions.

---

13. BT, 2015.

Here is one of the difficulties I have experienced with selling art online: Often times, a problem arises when customers do not read an auction completely, so they do not understand what they are buying. I find this happens less on my personal business site, although the auction listings contain same or similar information. I assume this has to do with the customer base viewing the material. With sites such as eBay, you have a wider demographic viewing your artwork than those looking at Artist-How-To.

I enjoy selling online because I prefer to work alone. I never have enjoyed dealing with people when selling my work. Selling online allows me to do what I love to do and not be concerned when selling if my hair is combed or if I am wearing the "right clothes." My shyness is so strong that if possible I would never deal with people at all. But it is necessary in order to do the job.

There is very little I dislike about selling art online, but I do have a difficult time shutting off work at the end of the day. I find my 'in-box' is always full. From marketing, developing ideas, organizing, or getting down to creating, there is always something that needs my attention.

If I had to start over again, I would be more open to asking and accepting help from others. I find that I want to do it all myself. I only recently hired someone to create a graphic I needed. For a while I had a studio assistant to handle jobs such as shipping, etc., but overall, I wish I was better at delegating.

If you are thinking of building a business selling creative works online, start out slow. Build a strong body of work before you concern yourself with having a site. Show only the very best work. Realize that doing art as a business is a juggling act. And remember it is a business. Keep good records of all expenses and income. If you are not sure what to keep track of, and you live in the U.S. get your hands on a Schedule C tax form as an example of where to begin. Seek out advice from the Small Business Administration at **www.sba.gov** and your state's Arts Commission.

Although many people look for the perfect way to promote their artworks, I do not think there is just one way or method. However, there are some that work substantially better than others. Join groups and network with those interested in possibly purchasing your work. Submit your site to search engines, trade links with other artists whose work you respect. Create a blog of interest to your customers to draw them to your site. Only later, after you have exhausted all free methods, should you even consider other methods.

Also, you do not have to wait for months for someone to come along and find your artwork; instead, you can create a work and have it sold and shipped to a buyer within a matter of days. Some artists who sell their works through auction listings can sell works as fast as they create them, which creates a constant source of revenue that traditional gallery artists are not able to enjoy.

FAST FACT

eBay has 25 million sellers and around 157 million buyers. [14]

How much can you make selling art on eBay? Art on eBay frequently sells from $40 to $700 per work. There are a number of artists who make six-figure salaries by selling art on eBay, and many others who have replaced their "day job" salaries with the income made from eBay sales.

As with any online marketing tool, you need to know and use specific strategies to successfully compete with the thousands of other artists who are selling their work. At any given time, there are thousands of original artworks for sale in the "Self-Representing Artists" category alone, and many other creative works for sale in other categories.

It's important to know how to craft great auction listings that attract visitors, capture interest, and compel shoppers to bid on your artwork.

Setting up your eBay account

Setting up an eBay account is a simple process. You will need to set up both a buyer's account and a seller's account to post auction listings. First go to

---

14. BT, 2015.

www.ebay.com and click on the "Register" link to begin setting up your account. You will need to include your name, email address, and phone number.

To create a basic buyer's account, you will also select a username for your account. Your username should reflect your business, and it can be the same as your website address.

After registering with eBay, you can create a seller's account by logging in to eBay and clicking the "Sellers" link on your "My eBay" page.

To create a seller's account, you will need to provide eBay with a credit card so you can be charged for the fees you incur from posting auction listings and selling your creative works. If you have a PayPal account, you can elect to have your seller's fees deducted from PayPal, but you will still need to provide a credit card as a backup. You can sell your works yourself or pay to have selling experts sell your work for you. There are a variety of selling options and fees, all of which are listed here: **http://pages.ebay.com/seller -center/stores/subscriptions.html**.

FAST FACT

The stock market value of eBay is $32 million.[15]

Listings and fees

You can list up to 50 items per month on eBay, and you only pay a 10 percent final valuation fee when your items sell. What you get is a chance to show your work to over 160 million shoppers. You'll also get shipping

---

15. BT, 2015.

labels that can be printed at home and discounts on postage. Additionally, you will receive seller protection and help with selling your stuff.

Reserve fees

If you want to make sure you get a good price for your creative work, you can place a reserve on your auction selling price. A reserve is a minimum price below which you are not obligated to sell your item. If the highest bid price for your item does not meet the reserve you have set, the highest bidder will not be entitled to your artwork.

You will still be charged listing fees for your auction, but setting a reserve can still be an effective way of making sure you do not sell your item for less than you spent creating and listing it.

If the highest bid exceeds the reserve you have set, you will be obligated to sell the item to the highest bidder.

Buy It Now fees

If you want to give your bidders the option to end the auction early by purchasing your artwork at a specific price, you can set a "Buy It Now" price for your auction. If you know you will have several bidders competing to win your auction, "Buy It Now" is a good tool to give yourself the chance to sell your creative work at your optimal price.

To find out more about the various fees and how they work, visit **http://pages.ebay.com/help/sell/fees.html**.

There are several other enhancements you can add to your auction listings. You can add a colored background or a border in the listing results to make your auction stand out; or you can place your auction in the "Featured Auctions" listings, which places your auction in front of all the standard listings, so yours will be among the first auctions visible when a user searches your category.

eBay charges for each of these features, so take time to determine how much you can spend on a listing and still have a good chance of making a profit from your auctions.

Building auction listings

Once you have created your seller's account, you are ready to start posting auction listings to sell your creative works. To begin building an auction listing, place your pointer over the "Sell" link at the top of your account page, and select "Sell an Item" from the drop-down menu.

You will then select the category and subcategory in which you would like your auction listing to appear. One of the most popular categories for artists and other creative people is "Self-Representing Artists." This is a good category if you are selling visual artwork such as paintings, sculptures, or photographs, because eBay buyers know they can find original art in this category rather than reproductions. You can also concurrently place your listing in another category, such as "Contemporary Art," to gain even more exposure for your listings.

Keep in mind, though, that if you concurrently list your item in two categories, eBay will charge you listing fees for each category, effectively doubling the amount you will pay for listing your auction on eBay.

Choosing the length and timing of your auctions

Before you compose an auction listing, you will need to decide a couple of important things—how long you want your auction to run and when you want it to end. Both factors can affect how many bids your auction receives and how high the final bid is.

eBay allows you to run an auction for one, three, five, seven, or 10 days. The listing template defaults to seven days, but you can shorten or lengthen this timeframe if you feel it will provide you with a competitive advantage. However, if you are using the fixed price format, where your goods are sold at a set price, you can also choose a 30-day or "Good 'Til Cancelled" listing duration.

Some artists choose one or three day listings to convey a sense of urgency among bidders. Bidders who view these listings know if they do not place their best bids right away, they will lose out on the chance to win the auction.

The auction title

When people search for an item on eBay, they use "keywords" to find what they are looking for, just like Internet users search for websites using keywords. eBay's search engine searches the titles and descriptions of every active auction to find those keywords and then provides a list of all auctions that contain the keywords.

You have less than 100 characters available, so every single word must work to bring in traffic and catch the reader's attention. Come up with a title that is descriptive, keyword searchable, and easily identifies you.

The auction design

The next step in creating a superior auction is the design of the auction listing itself. Many sellers simply use eBay's default auction template, which creates a uniform layout.

However, you can use auction template generators to add visual interest to your listings. A free and highly versatile auction template builder is available at **www.robshelp.com**. You can add multiple images, customize the layout of your auction listing, and select unique fonts for your listing text to make your auctions stand out from those of your competitors.

An auction template builder can help you easily add lots of things to make your listings stand out, like textured backgrounds, multiple photos of your art, and unique fonts. You are essentially creating a webpage out of your auction listing that will grab the buyer's attention and keep them focused on your listing.

Once you have created a design that is uniquely your own, utilize the same design for every auction. This creates a sort of "branding" tool that lets buyers know whose art they are looking at before they read a word of the auction listing. Also, make sure it looks similar to your other online stores.

The auction text

Buyers not only want to see pictures of your art, they want to "know" about it. Take the time to describe the artwork you are selling. How big is it? What colors were used? Is it smooth and sleek, or is it heavily textured? You may assume that buyers can see all of these things in the auction photos, but differences in monitor settings and quality can hide or distort these details in even the best photos. Since you do not have any control over this, you need to provide these details in words as well as in pictures.

In addition, it is important to include information about what the artwork means to you. What inspired the work? What were you thinking when you created the art? Was there some unique experience that made you hopelessly, obsessively compelled to put your thoughts and emotions about the experience on canvas? Buyers like to know what a piece of art means to the artist.

Your "About Me" page

Although this is not technically part of any one auction listing, it is a part of your profile that can be accessed from every listing that you post on eBay.

This section includes not only text but also photos of yourself hard at work in your studio, examples from your art portfolio, and information on how to contact you directly. Use this space to your fullest advantage by also including your artist's statement, some highlights of your career as an artist, and, most importantly, the link to your individual artist website or other sites you want to list where your buyers can find out more about you and your work.

Unfortunately, eBay does not allow you to link directly to your website from your auction listings. On your "About Me" page, though, it is permissible to include a link to your website.

Also, don't forget to include your studio logo that you made when you were building your individual artist website.

Your auction price

The typical logic dictates that your starting bid price should be the minimum amount of money that you would be comfortable selling your artwork for. Of course, to determine this figure, you need to keep track of how much you spent on materials for a piece of art, how many hours you spent creating it, and how much you are investing in eBay listing fees. You might also look at what other artists who are selling similar work are charging.

If you browse through a few eBay listings, you will undoubtedly notice there are quite a few that start out at a nominal bid (usually $1). This is a popular tactic used by new auction marketers. They figure that the low starting price will entice bids, and once people start bidding, the listing will attract more attention and bidders will get into a sort of "bidding war" that will culminate in a high closing bid.

However, the only artists that can get away with this are the ones who have already developed a following they can count on to bid no matter what they produce. It can take years to develop that kind of following, and unless you have this sort of loyal clientele, using this technique is not recommended. You may end up giving away a valuable artwork for $1.

CASE STUDY: TANYA BOND

www.tanyabond.com
http://stores.ebay.com/Tanyas-Irish-Art
http://www.tanyabond.etsy.com/

I started as a buyer on eBay, and then I realized that I might try to sell my art and it worked slowly but surely. Right now about 80 percent of my sales are done online. I have only sold from my website 2 times so far, so my online business is mostly concentrated on eBay and a bit on ETSY. I believe having a blog helps generate extra visibility.

One of the few difficulties I have experienced with selling art online is that sometimes people prefer large artwork or framed under glass, which can easily be damaged while posted.

To me, the best thing about selling art online is surprise - the sales normally come when you least expect them. Also there is no shop/gallery set up cost, no need to look after it - so what you gain is a lot of free time that can be spent on creating more art. And huge audiences can be reached when selling online and it's quite flattering to know that your works are being kept in collections all over the world.

If I had to start over again, I would not underprice my work from the very start. And I also would not get frustrated over very little sales in comparison with some established online sellers.

My best advice for people new to selling creative works online is this -- do not expect miracles, generally it takes several months if not years to get established online.

Your eBay store

In addition to auction listings, you can also sell creative works in your eBay store. An eBay store allows you to list hundreds of items for sale at once and categorize each item to help users find your store items. The fees for listing these items are much lower than the fees for launching auctions, so you can make a greater profit from your eBay store items than through auction items.

There are three store types: Basic, Premium, and Anchor. Each of these plans offers monthly and yearly subscription fees. To find out the current plans and fees, visit http://pages.ebay.com/seller-center/stores/subscriptions.html.

Your eBay store listings will show up in your active auctions, which creates an effective cross selling tool to help you sell more artwork and develop long-term relationships with your clients.

Artsy

Artsy is also an option for online auctioning. However, unlike eBay, Artsy focuses on high-end artwork sales and auctions. Their database of 350,000 images features art, design, photography, sculptures, prints, and more by over 50,000 artists. It a place to go to get inspired, learn about art, and further appreciate art, even if you are not yet qualified to show and sell your work on Artsy.

To sell your art on Artsy, you have to be affiliated with a partner gallery that works with Artsy. This site is changing the way fine art is bought, sold, and discovered. There are several hundred thousand registered users in several hundred countries. It's not even easy for a gallery to sell on Artsy. In fact, there is a waiting list. However, stick with creating your artwork, and you may someday be a part of this high-end online gallery that was created for the world's best artwork. Find out more at **www.artsy.net**.

CHAPTER 10

Connecting to Your Customers Through Email

L ike with any business, it's important to keep in touch with your customers. You can do this through email and social media outlets and through more traditional means such as mail and newsletters. In this chapter, we will look at these ways to connect to your customers.

Even if you're not a writer, there are places to go for writing help and advice. We will discuss this in more detail in this chapter and in Chapter 12. In Chapter 11, we will learn about using autoresponder services to create opt-in forms for your website and manage email messages to people who subscribe to your email list.

Email

No matter how well you have designed your website, or how tempting your product selection is, you are competing with all the other things that vie for your visitors' attention. If you give your visitors the opportunity to subscribe to your email marketing list, which we cover in Chapter 11, you will be able to frequently remind them of your products, so that when they find a time free from distractions, they will be able to return to your website and purchase your creative works.

Email marketing also works because it gives you the opportunity to provide your subscribers with relevant, useful information that will give them an educational and entertaining break from their day-to-day tasks. It also establishes you as an authority in your field, because you will be the one who will provide information that is readily visible to your subscribers.

By sending frequent emails about your products and different art-related topics, or even images of new pieces, your subscribers will come to trust you as an expert on your style of art. Your email can be in the form of a written note and can even have an attachment, such as a flyer. The flyer could have information about your new pieces, pictures of your work, and your contact information. Keep the look, tone, and feel consistent with your other social media accounts and websites.

You can find flyer templates at **https://templates.office.com**. Also, many word processing programs have built in templates.

Finally, email marketing works because your subscribers feel special when they receive promotional offers and discounts from you that you do not offer non-subscribers. They can be the first to know about new artwork you have completed, and you can even tell them about special creative works and projects that are not available to the public. By giving your subscribers a sense of exclusivity, you will build a loyal client base who will buy from you more often.

Email mini courses

Creating an email mini course is an excellent way to continuously remind your subscribers about your business, because you can spend a few hours creating a course and put it to work for you for years to come. This can be a YouTube video you have made, or even a podcast, which we discussed in Chapter 8.

As a creative person, what knowledge could you share through an email course that would benefit your subscribers? No matter what types of creative works you are selling, you have special knowledge that could benefit your readers. For example, if you are a visual artist—say, a landscape painter—you could easily create an email course instructing subscribers on how to correctly hang and display paintings.

To get the maximum exposure from your email mini course, divide the material you want to cover into several parts. Using the above example, you could come up with at least six parts for your "How to Hang and Display Paintings" email course:

- Selecting Correctly Sized Artwork for Your Room

- Choosing Landscape or Portrait Oriented Paintings

- Selecting the Right Hanging Hardware for Your Art

- How to Install Hanging Hardware on Your Artwork

- Selecting the Correct Height for Your Paintings

- How to Space Your Artwork to Avoid the Sense of Clutter

Once you have decided on your subtopics for your email course, use your autoresponder service to draft emails that will contain the material covered in your course. Using the "How to Hang and Display Paintings" example, you would draft a total of eight emails — one introducing the subscriber to the course and telling him or her about what can be expected from the course, one for each of the six parts of the course, and one thanking the subscriber for reading the course and inviting him or her to visit your website or blog for more art-related information.

Your emails should be written in a conversational tone. You want your subscribers to be entertained as well as educated by your course, so you will want to keep it as light as possible.

Each email should include a short blurb containing your website address and an invitation to visit your online gallery. It does not have to be anything elaborate; it can be a simple line or two like, "Joe Smith has been creating art and helping clients display their artworks for over a decade. To find out more about Joe's artworks, visit **www.joesmithartstudio.com**."

Be sure to use your final email to not only thank your subscribers for taking the course and invite them to browse your gallery, but also to tell them about other free courses you offer. If a subscriber signs up for another course, you will have several more opportunities to contact your client and invite them to browse and purchase your creative works.

Once you have written all the emails for your mini course, load them into your autoresponder and set each email to go out on a different day, perhaps every other day. By using an autoresponder service to do this, you don't have to worry about remembering to send out the parts of your email course to subscribers at the appropriate times. Once you have set up your emails in the autoresponder, it will automatically send out each email at the intervals you specify. This is a great way to promote your business without adding hours of work to your schedule each day.

How do email courses help you promote your business? Statistics show that on average, you will need to make a contact with a potential client seven times before he or she makes a purchase.

Newsletters

Newsletters are an excellent way to maintain contact with your subscribers without making them feel like you are trying to sell them something. Your newsletters can highlight a new art series you have started, tell your readers about a charity event to which you have donated creative works, or show images from a recent gallery showing that featured your art. You can also use newsletters to provide informative articles that your readers can use when selecting and purchasing creative works.

Depending on the scale of your business, you may have enough material to send out a monthly newsletter. If not, a bi-monthly or quarterly newsletter is fine. You should have enough material to keep your readers interested for a while and plenty of images to showcase your creative works.

When creating your newsletter, make sure the layout and color scheme match your website as closely as possible and include your business logo if you have one. Doing this will help build branding, which we covered in Chapter 2. People should see your logo and your page layout and immediately know who the email is from.

It is important to make your newsletters look as professional as possible. Even though you are using your newsletters to inform and entertain your readers, you are also building a professional image with these emails. A well-designed newsletter will show your subscribers that you are a professional and that you take your business seriously.

Most autoresponders will let you set up and send HTML emails so your newsletter can mirror the design of your website. However, not all email applications can correctly display HTML emails, so it is a good idea to put the newsletter on your website and provide a link in your email for people who cannot display HTML messages.

There are a few places you can find newsletter templates, such as Pinterest and Google Docs. Remember to find one that you like and use it each time for consistency.

Also, be sure to keep your look, style, and tone similar to your other online efforts, like your website, blog, and social media pages.

Never share email addresses with others

It can be tempting to share the email addresses you gather through your marketing efforts, either for profit or to join forces with another artist so you can both have larger subscriber lists. However, this is a bad idea, and it can cause significant damage to your reputation and your business.

First, selling or otherwise giving the email addresses of your subscribers to someone else without their consent violates federal privacy laws and can cause you to incur stiff fines. Second, it erodes the trust of your customers. No one wants to receive scores of emails from people they do not know because you sold or gave away their email address. Once you sell or give away an address, you have no control over how another person chooses to use it. So, don't do it.

Update your email list

As you get new requests from your website to add someone to your email list, try to do it as soon as possible. Once subscribers are on board and begin to feel connected to you as an artist, you will have a better chance of making an art sale. Also, if you have a customer that has requested to be taken off your mail list, take care of this right away. Don't take it personally. They may get too many emails and not have time to read them all.

Getting Writing Help

Even if you are not a great writer, don't worry. There are ways you can polish up your thoughts and brush on your grammar without spending an arm and a leg. You can try to find someone you know to help you formulate your thoughts or even proofread. That someone can be a friend, a family member, or someone you know from school.

Don't forget that you can use your own grammar and spellchecker that come with most word processing programs. Double check any words that you are unsure of in a dictionary. Alternative words can be found in a thesaurus. You might also check for editors and proofreaders on Craigslist. (However, if you do, first review What to Watch Out for When Selling Online in Chapter 8.)

You can also hire someone to write something for you. These writers can assist with email messages, newsletters, website content, and even with keyword optimization at reasonable rates.

Upwork

A good website for finding freelance writers to create your website and blog content is **www.upwork.com**. There are thousands of freelance writers from dozens of countries that specialize in creating website, blog, and article copy. Many of these writers also understand the content strategies required to obtain excellent search engine rankings, so investing in a freelance writer will not only help you get website content that your visitors will enjoy, it will also help you rank high in search engine listings without requiring you to spend long evenings trying to learn the nuances of website optimization. Upwork offers a helpful guide that details all the steps needed to find a writer though their service. Everything from creating your job post to finding the right person to hire is covered in the guide.

Other Freelance Writer Websites

There are dozens of other websites you can use to find a freelance writer to provide content for your website, articles, or blog posts. You can check **www.freelancewriting.com**, **www.writeraccess.com,** and **www.guru.com** for experienced writers. Many freelance writing websites allow buyers to post projects for free. Check under their help section for details.

Now that you have learned how to create email courses and newsletters to promote your business and retain the interest of your opt-in subscribers, as well as found out where you can turn to for writing help, let's move on to the next chapter, where you will learn what types of software can help best ensure your business success.

CHAPTER 11

Software and Sites That Offer the Tools for Success

To sell a creative work online, you will need to a way of receiving payment from your customer. This chapter will briefly outline some of the considerations for taking care of this task as well as offer advice about other important financial tools for success, such as software programs related to tracking, accounting, and business plans. Also, there are a variety of software programs that were designed to help you do everything from retouch photos to edit videos. We'll also discuss those types of software tools.

Payment for Your Items

Before your customers purchase your works, you should let them know what payment methods are available. Many Internet users assume that if they are purchasing something online, they will be able to make payment with a credit card on the website they purchased the item from. If you do not accept credit cards on your website, make this clear on your website or auction listing.

In the following sections, we will discuss the most common payment methods you can make available to your customers.

Credit card payments made directly on your website

This method is the most convenient for your customers. They can enter their credit card numbers on the ordering page, click the submit button, and complete their transactions in just a minute or two.

Offering this payment is a little more complicated for website owners. First, you must purchase a merchant account with the ability to process online transactions. A merchant account is a special bank account used to accept credit card payment from consumers. When you apply for a merchant account, it will be underwritten just like any other type of financial account. The company offering the merchant account will evaluate your business, the amount of transactions it anticipates that you will generate, and the condition of your own credit.

It can cost several hundred dollars to set up a merchant account and integrate it into your website. Plus, there may be monthly fees that come with the account. You also have to make sure the payment authorization interface used by the merchant account company is compatible with the shopping cart software used by your website's hosting company, if your hosting company offers a shopping cart feature. Be sure to check with the help center of the website host that you are using.

Merchant account providers charge fees for each transaction that is processed, in addition to any setup or maintenance fees. Transaction fees are usually between two and four percent of the total purchase price, depending on the provider and the type of merchant account you select. Some providers charge by transaction, while others charge by the month.

Unless you are selling a large volume of artwork on your website, it may make better sense to use PayPal.

PayPal

With PayPal, you can still accept payments by credit card, but customers will be redirected to a PayPal page to enter their payment information.

PayPal is substantially easier to use than a merchant account because you don't have to worry about integrating anything or setting up a virtual shopping cart on your website. You can simply copy a snippet of HTML code available when you register for your free account at **www.paypal.com** and paste it into your website to give your customers the ability to pay you through PayPal. PayPal offers helpful information on how to do this at their on-site "Getting Started Center."

When payments are made through PayPal, the funds are deposited into an account available on your secure PayPal page. You can withdraw these funds to your own personal checking or savings account for free. It usually takes three or four business days for the funds to appear in your personal account.

You can also get a reloadable PayPal debit card, which will allow you to make purchases at any retailer that accepts credit cards, and debit the funds from your PayPal balance. This can be a good way to keep your personal and business finances separate. You can use PayPal to pay for supplies, website hosting, shipping, and other costs related to your business, instead of using your personal checking account.

Like merchant accounts, PayPal charges a percentage of the total amount of each payment you receive, plus a nominal processing fee. Currently, 2.9 percent of each transaction, plus an additional $0.30 for processing, is deducted from each payment that is deposited into your PayPal account.

PayPal also allows you to accept funds via electronic checks, or eChecks. To you, there is virtually no difference between receiving a payment funded by a credit card and a payment funded by an electronic check except that it may take a few days for an electronic check to clear, so you may not have immediate access to those funds.

Checks and money orders

You can also offer to accept payment via a personal check or money order mailed to you.

However, if you allow a customer to pay by personal check or money order, you will not only have to wait for the check to arrive in the mail, you will also have to wait for the check to clear. If it does not clear, then you are stuck trying to collect the returned check fee charged by your bank, in addition to the purchase price of your artwork.

If you *do* decide to accept personal checks, it is important that you do not ship the artwork until the payment clears. If you have already shipped the item before a customer's check is returned for insufficient funds, you may have a difficult time collecting valid payment from that customer.

Software and Web Services for Running Your Business

Now we will discuss the tools that you can use to build your business more quickly and easily, while saving money and frustration along the way. Some of these tools can be acquired as your business begins to generate a profit; others are essential to getting started.

Website creation tools

Unless you use a template-based site builder offered by your website host (easier) or you have extensive knowledge of website coding languages, such as HTML and JavaScript (harder), you will need a website creation tool to properly design your site and make sure all the elements of your site are functional. There are several website creation tools available that can make designing your website a simple and relatively quick process. However, keep in mind that many website hosts, such as **www.weebly.com** and **www.godaddy.com**, offer their own tools.

Adobe Dreamweaver CC

Adobe Dreamweaver CC, an all-in-one visual development tool that is used to create, manage, and publish websites, is a good choice. This website creation tool is designed to be compatible with both Windows-based systems and Macintosh systems. If you purchase Adobe Dreamweaver CC directly from the manufacturer's website at **www.adobe.com/products /dreamweaver**, you can expect to pay about $600 for this software; however, you can also pay for it by the month. You can also find Dreamweaver CC on **www.amazon.com** for as little as $240 per year with a 12-month plan.

The program is available as a seven day trial download if you want to give it a spin before purchasing.

PageBreeze

PageBreeze, powered by Microsoft Internet Explorer, is another way to build your website. PageBreeze is a free website creation tool available for download at **www.pagebreeze.com**.

There are no time restrictions or hidden fees associated with your Page-Breeze download. You can use the free software as long as you want and build as many websites and web pages as you want. The software is not as sophisticated as Dreamweaver CC, but it gives you the ability to build your website via both a WYSIWYG (visual) interface and HTML tag/source modes. A preview mode allows you to see what you have built before it's published. Pus, there are a variety of website templates to choose from.

PageBreeze can be an economical way to design your website and achieve professional results. One thing to note is that, according to their site, "If you use PageBreeze in your job, or in a for-profit business for non-evaluation purposes, you must obtain an inexpensive license for PageBreeze Professional, which includes many more advanced features."

CGI Form and Autoresponder Tools

It's important to remind your visitors of your presence and entice them to return to your website through discounts, special offers, and announcements of your new creative works, all of which were discussed in Chapters 4, 5, and 6. The easiest way to do this is to provide a way for your website visitors to enter their email addresses on your site and to compile these email addresses into marketing lists so you can create email announcements.

CGI forms

A CGI form is a text field you can place on your website so that your visitors can enter their contact details or other information. You can use CGI forms to ask visitors for their names, email addresses, telephone numbers, favorite types of artwork, or any other information you can use in your marketing efforts.

Once a website visitor has entered his or her contact information into a CGI form on your website, it will be transmitted to a CGI bin, which formats the information submitted by the visitor and sends it to your email address. You can then transfer the information to a database, which you can use to easily send email messages to an entire group of people with just the click of a mouse.

Because federal laws prohibit the use of spam or transmission of unsolicited email messages, you should always couple CGI forms with a pre-written email requiring visitors to confirm they have voluntarily submitted their contact information and that they consent to receiving email messages from you. Many web hosts offer forms that you can personalize based on your own needs, such as what type of information that your customer provides—like name and email.

Autoresponders

Autoresponders are email programs that allow you to compose emails and have them sent as soon as a visitor completes a CGI form on your website (and at specified time intervals thereafter). This can save you lots of time, because you can set up your email messages once and never have to worry about checking for new subscribers and manually sending them emails.

There are several applications that can help you place CGI forms on your website and automatically send email messages to your subscribers. The following autoresponders can be used to promote your artwork, announce discounts and specials, and provide your subscribers with useful information to establish your position as a professional artist.

FormBreeze

FormBreeze is a CGI form generator and autoresponder system that is designed to be used with the PageBreeze website creation tool and work with your already-created website. FormBreeze allows you to easily create visitor input forms for use on your website, and it provides unlimited autoresponders to send email messages to subscribers that complete your web forms.

You can customize your autoresponder messages to be sent at specified intervals. For example, you may create a confirmation email that will be sent as soon as a visitor completes a CGI web form, or a welcome message that will be sent as soon as the visitor confirms his or her subscription, or sales emails every other day for the next two weeks to help familiarize your subscriber with your creative works. You can also create broadcast emails that will be sent to all your current subscribers at once so you can alert them of new artwork or discounts that will only be available for a limited time.

FormBreeze allows you to collect statistics about your subscribers, such as the percentage of subscribers that open an autoresponder email, the number of subscribers that click on a link contained in an email, and the number of people that unsubscribe from your mailing lists. This can help you understand how well your email marketing efforts are working, so you can adjust future email campaigns. FormBreeze also offers a free, 7-day trial period, and $7.95 per month for up to 3 forms or $19.95 per month for up to 10 forms thereafter.

AWeber

AWeber is another tool you can use consider as it makes it easy to create automated emails, build mobile response sign up forms, assist with collecting subscribers for your email list, and more. You can try AWeber for free for 30 days, and after that, it's $19.99 per month for unlimited emails and up to 500 subscribers. Find out more at **www.aweber.com**.

GetResponse

GetResponse offers many of the same features and tools as AWeber and FormBreeze. With packages starting at $15 a month, you can easily create email marketing, landing pages, and more.

Visitor Tracking Software

If you want your website to be a success and generate sufficient sales to derive a full-time income from your creative works online, you will need to have a means to determine how well your website is performing. There are several tools you can use to analyze the traffic on your website so you can predict your site's success and make modifications to increase its performance.

StatCounter

StatCounter is a free tool you can use to analyze the traffic on your website and learn how you can improve your website's content to generate additional traffic. You can register for a free account at **www.statcounter.com**. The registration process takes just a few minutes. You will enter your contact information and a few details about your website, and you will have access to several features that can help you determine the success of your site. You can track customer activity in real time, optimize design and content, and more.

OneStatFree

Another free website traffic analysis tool is available at **www.onestatfree .com**. Like StatCounter, you can see how many people have visited your site, find out which of your web pages are most popular, see which browsers your visitors are using most, and more. You can register for a free hit counter on their site, and they have upgrades available with different paid packages.

Photo Editing and Video Editing Tools

Photo editing

As you create pictures for your website and blog, you may be able to enhance them with photo editing tools. You can add creative effects, do retouching, lighten and darken images, and more. Other programs you might consider are Adobe Photoshop CC, which costs about $79 per month as an annual plan if you pay per month. You can find Adobe Photoshop CC here: **www.adobe.com/products/photoshop.html**. However, sites like **www.pizlr.com**, **www.picmonkey.com**, and **www.photoscape .com** offer free image editing tools.

Video editing

If you are looking for video editing tools for those "how-to" videos or introductory videos we discussed in Chapters 7 & 8, you have a few options. If you have a Mac and can spare the cash, you can get Apple Final Cut Pro X for $299. If you're a PC user, you might check out Corel VideoStudio Ultimate X9 for $69.

Of course, there are also plenty of free options out there, such as Lightworks at **www.lightworks.com**, Avidemux at **http://fixounet.free.fr/avidemux**, and VSDC Free Video Editor at **www.videosoftdev.com/free-video-editor**.

Most video editing software takes a powerful computer to run, so it's a good idea to check system requirements before purchasing or downloading anything.

Accounting and financial tools

One of the crucial elements of building a successful business is the ability to effectively manage your business's money. Profitable businesses must account for marketing, inventory, material, and other expenses, while also pricing products to provide revenue over these expenses. The following tools can help you manage your business's finances so you can reduce expenses and maximize profit.

Quicken

Quicken is a financial management software tool that you can use to make sure your business stays profitable. Quicken will easily handle many of the elements required to keep your creative business financially sound. You can purchase Quicken for both Mac and PC at http://quicken.intuit.com, with a starter version that is $39.99.

GnuCash

GnuCash is a free alternative to Quicken. When you download the software from **www.gnucash.org**, you will have access to many tools that will allow you to effectively manage your personal and business finances.

Mint

Mint is an easy-to-use software that allows you to bring all your finances together in one place. You can sign up for free, and you can sync your bank account. Check it out at **www.mint.com/how-mint-works**.

Money Manager

Money Manager is also a free and easy-to-use personal finance software that provides helpful tools and features. You can find out more at **www .moneymanagerex.org**.

Business Plan Tools

A business plan is essential if you want to plan for the growth and success of your business. It's also necessary if you ever decide to pursue a loan to finance future expansion of your business. You can access resources that will provide you with sample plans for a variety of business types and give you templates that you can use to create your own business plan.

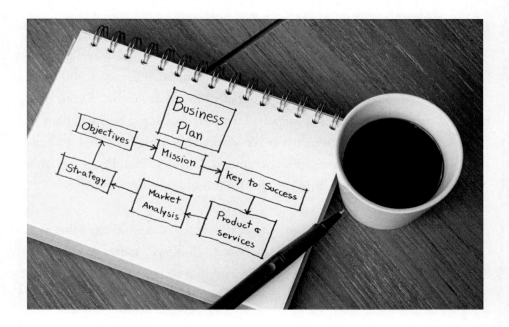

BPlans

At www.bplans.com, you can choose from over 500 free sample business plans. These plans represent a wide variety of styles and provide samples of plans for various industries. The site also offers many articles that cover different aspects of your plan, giving you advice about what types of information to include and how to present the information so that your business vision will be communicated clearly and effectively to potential investors, loan officers, and other people who will have the power to influence the success of your business and help you reach your financial and career goals.

Additionally, you'll find several calculators that you can use to calculate startup costs, determine when your business will break even, and even determine the return on investment you can expect from paid advertising efforts such as pay-per-click marketing.

Business Plan Pro

If you need additional assistance to create a business plan, you may consider purchasing Business Plan Pro. This software includes over 500 business plan samples and gives you a number of templates to build your own plan. It also provides step-by-step assistance in creating a business plan so you can make sure all elements of your business are considered and included in your final business plan document. Business Plan Pro is available at **www.bplans.com/mk/bpp_jp.cfm** for a standard plan of $99.95.

Now that we have reviewed some of the software and online tools that you might consider for your online business, we will discuss where to turn to if you need help with anything from web building to connecting with other artists.

CHAPTER 12

Where to Turn When You Need Help

As with anything, when it comes to selling your artwork online, there's a learning curve. There may be times when you need to reach out for extra help. You may need help with website building, understanding how to set up your business, or connecting to others who have similar goals as you do. In this final chapter, we will go over a few ideas about where you can turn to for help.

Need Help Learning the Skills to Set up Your New Business?

There's no doubt about it, setting up a business is a daunting task. Whether you are trying to set up a web page or determining the best way to market your business, there's no shame in asking for a little guidance. We've compiled a list of some general resources that will be beneficial to you as you begin the exciting journey of becoming an entrepreneur!

On-site classes

Check your local library, parks and recreation department, community college, and technical school for affordable classes in web building, design, photography, and other technical areas that may apply to your goal of selling artwork online. Many offer introductory classes in web design, graphic design, and business. Topics range from marketing and bookkeeping to basic HTML and typography.

On-site groups

You might also find a meetup group in your area focused on technology, design, and business that is dedicated to learning new skills and brushing up on the ones they already know. Plus, joining a group is a chance to network with people who have similar interests and goals. Meetup groups are generally free to join, and sometimes there is a nominal fee. Either way, it's worth checking out. Find one in your area at **www.meetup.com**.

YouTube

YouTube is a great place to find information and mini lectures about many issues, such as how to build a website, use Photoshop, or market your business. Log into YouTube and conduct a search at **www.youtube.com**.

Khan Academy

Khan Academy offers a variety of classes, such as those pertaining to digital camera, web site building, and more—all for free. Find out more at **www.khanacademy.org**.

Lynda.com

Lynda is where many professionals turn to learn new skills and brush up on the ones they already have. From management to basic InDesign, Lynda has it all. If you're interested, sign up for the free 10-day trial. If you decide this is the site for you, here are various plans to fit your needs. Find out more at **www.lynda.com**.

Small Business Administration (SBA)

The Small Business Administration offers many online classes for free, such as "Understanding Your Customer" and "Competitive Advantage." Find out more at **www.sba.gov**. You can also check out their YouTube channel at **www.youtube.com/user/sba**.

Need Help Connecting to Other Artists?

While you may already have artist friends and fellow classmates that you can turn to for advice, bounce ideas off of, or enjoy artistic events with, there are other places you can look for like-minded people.

Online groups

You might find a group of like-minded artists at your school, place of worship, or club you belong to. Your group might connect via their own Facebook page or they might have a meetup group. Other considerations are groups at Deviant Art: http://groups.deviantart.com, The Art Colony: **http://theartcolony.ning.com**, Fine Art America: **https://fineartamerica.com/groups**, and Pixels: **https://pixels.com/groups.html**

On-Site groups

Meetup groups are also a great resource for connecting with fellow artists. Get inspired, learn some new skills, and make friends at **www.meetup.com**.

There are even more ways to connect to others, such as attending local art events, stopping by a gallery or museum to see their new exhibit, attending places of worship, and more. It's important to network as much as you can to really get your business booming, and that includes on-site and online activities. Hopefully, this book brought you one step closer to reaching your goal as a successful artist.

Conclusion

Throughout the pages of this book, you have learned how to build an online business to promote and sell your artwork. By now, you should have the resources you need to build a profitable and rewarding online business. Like any business, selling art online is neither easy nor free of frustrations. However, if you follow the steps described in this book, you will have a much greater chance of success than most people who only dream of making a living from their creative works.

Keep this book close at hand while you are building your art business. You will want to refer to it often for tips on how to display, market, sell, and distribute your creative works. Remember, you *can* have success as an artist and you *can* make a living selling your work online. Best of luck!

About the Author

Ann M. O'Phelan has a B.A. in business and advertising and an M.F.A. in creative writing. She is also an artist who especially enjoys acrylic painting.

Glossary

Affiliate link: A link contained on a website that directs a visitor to another website offering products or services for sale. A website owner who places an affiliate link on his or her site has previously entered an agreement with the website offering the products or services, which allows the referring website owner to earn a portion of sales derived from the referral. Affiliate links contain a unique identifier that helps the product site owner track referrals and pay commissions to affiliates.

Affiliate marketing: Affiliate marketing involves enlisting other Internet marketers to generate interest for your website and sending visitors to you so they can view and purchase your artwork, crafts, photographs, or music.

Affiliate program: A revenue sharing program used by Internet marketers to increase sales or to gain income from referring buyers to another website offering products or services for sale. Website owners who sell products or services on a website may offer affiliates a percentage of any sales derived from a referral provided by the affiliate.

Alt tag: A short block of text associated with an image placed on a website. Website owners use alt tags to provide a short description of the image and most include keywords in the description to boost a web page's ranking in search engine listings for specific keywords.

Article directories: Websites that accept, categorize, and publish article content written and submitted by individual authors. Website owners write articles for publication and submission to article directories, and users can select articles from a directory for publication on their own websites. Article directories allow website owners to gain additional exposure for their web pages.

Article marketing: A marketing strategy in which a website owner writes free, informative articles and submits them to article directories for publication. Although article authors do not derive income directly from these articles, the authors benefit by including their website addresses and biographical information in the resource boxes that appear at the end of each article.

Artist group: An online gathering place for artists, crafters, photographers, or other creative professionals. Artist groups typically utilize discussion boards, chat rooms, and other means for artists to share ideas, participate in contests, and collaborate on creative works. Artist groups also allow an artist to create a profile that can be used to promote creative works on other websites.

Auction listing: A specific page on eBay or other auction site that users can visit to learn about and place bids on an item you have posted for sale. Auction listings for creative works such as paintings, sculpture, handmade crafts, and photographs typically contain one or more images of the work, as well as a text description to describe the size of the work, the materials used in its construction, and other information to build interest and entice users to bid on the item.

Autoresponder: A software program or web-based application that allows you to compose and send emails to email marketing subscribers at specified intervals. Emails can be sent to all your email list subscribers at once or can be triggered by a website visitor's completion and submission of a CGI form. Autoresponders can save Internet markets a substantial amount of time by managing promotional emails without constant monitoring.

Bandwidth: The total size of files that are transferred when each website visitor accesses a web page or downloads files from a page. The larger the files on a website, the greater the bandwidth used to display those files on a visitor's Internet browser. Hosting providers place a monthly limit on the amount of bandwidth that can be generated by visitors accessing a website and charge the website owners overage fees when bandwidth is exceeded during a given month.

Blog: Short for web log. In its most rudimentary form, a blog is a series of text entries similar to a diary. Entries can be displayed in chronological or reverse chronological order. Blogs are used by businesses to promote products or services, as well as by personal users to keep family or friends up to date. Bloggers can integrate blogs into websites or create separate blogs that contain links and references to the websites.

Blogrings: On most blogging sites, blogs are divided into categories and subcategories according to the main theme or topic of each blog. Blogrings are groups of blogs that share a common theme, interest, or predominant topic.

Brand: A brand is a name, term, design, symbol, look, style, tone, or other feature that distinguishes one seller's product from others.

Broadcast email: An email sent to all subscribers at one time. Broadcast emails may be used to send special information or to alert subscribers to special offers or discounts on products available on the sender's website.

Browser: An interface that allows website visitors to access and view web pages on a personal computer. Different browsers can display web pages differently, so when a website owner is creating pages for his or her site, it is important for the owner to ensure the pages will display correctly on commonly used browsers. Common browsers include Internet Explorer, Netscape, Safari, and Mozilla Firefox.

Business plan: A detailed document that describes a business, identifies its owners and key personnel, and outlines the plans the business owners have for future growth. This document is necessary for business owners who wish to attract potential investors or business loans from financial institutions. It is also a valuable document for people just starting a business because it gives them a detailed blueprint to follow as the business grows and encounters new challenges.

Common Gateway Interface (CGI) form: A series of text boxes placed on a website to gather information about a website visitor. CGI forms can capture a visitor's name, email address, artistic preferences, or any other information an artist wishes to use to decide how to promote his or her creative works. Information entered into a CGI form by a website visitor is processed and sent to the artist's email inbox.

Computer processor unit (or CPU): The CPU is the electronic circuitry in a computer. The circuitry carries out the instructions of a computer program by performing the basic arithmetic, logical, control and input/output (I/O) operations that are specified by the instructions.

Discussion board: A section of a website where users can post thoughts, opinions, news, or other content about a particular subject. Other users may then respond to these messages, creating an asynchronous discussion that may go on for several pages. Discussion boards may contain hundreds or thousands of discussions.

DMOZ: DMOZ allows one to contribute to the accuracy of the web by porting issues, suggesting new sites for a specific category and volunteering to edit a specific category. As an editor, one can become recognized as an expert of your given topic.

Domain: The root address under which all pages of a website are grouped. A domain must be purchased or otherwise reserved by a website owner before a website can be published to the Internet. If an artist chooses the domain name **www.joesmithartgallery.com**, all pages of the website will use this domain as the root of its URL. Examples: **www.joesmithartgallery.com/home**, **www.joesmithartgallery.com/paintings**, **www.joesmithart gallery.com/contact_me**.

E-Commerce: E-Commerce s the transaction of buying or selling something online.

Email course: An instructional email designed to improve readers' knowledge about a topic related to the sender's website or business. Email courses may consist of a single email transmission or may be broken into several parts sent at designated intervals to give the sender more opportunities to contact the subscriber and remind him or her of products or information available on the web site.

Email marketing: An Internet marketing technique by which a website owner promotes his or her products via emails sent to newsletter subscribers. Purely informational emails may also be sent to build subscriber trust and loyalty. A website visitor must voluntarily offer his or her email address before the website owner can legally include the visitor in an email marketing campaign.

File transfer: The amount of bandwidth that is used when a visitor accesses web pages and downloads files contained on a website. Hosting providers place a limit on the amount of file transfer on a website every month and charge additional fees when file transfer exceeds the hosting plan's monthly allotment. A website owner who expects many visitors each month should purchase a hosting package that provides a generous bandwidth allotment to avoid overage charges.

Financial management software: Applications that allow a user to collect and synthesize data from personal checking, savings, investment, and business accounts and analyze the data to make sure that personal and business finances are sound. Some financial management software programs also allow users to manage business functions such as invoicing, payroll, taxes, and customer and vendor tracking.

Hard drive: Hardware in a personal computer or server where data is stored, such as word processor documents, media files, software files, and browser cookies. The capacity of a hard drive is expressed in gigabytes. The higher the capacity of a hard drive, the more data can be stored on it. A large capacity hard drive is essential for computers that will store large numbers of image or media files.

Hardware: Physical parts of a computer that provide various functions to make the computer operate correctly. Examples of hardware include hard drives, memory cards, processors, video cards, sound cards, CD and DVD drives, and motherboards.

High speed Internet access: Internet access that is transmitted over a cable line or via satellite.

Hosting Provider: A hosting provider is a company that places your website files on its servers (computers that hold a very large amount of information) and allows visitors to access your website through its servers. It is essentially a place where you go to rent out your web space.

Hyper Text Markup Language (HTML): A coding language used to create web pages. HTML uses tags to tell web browsers how to display website content. Popular website creation software automatically creates HTML as users build web pages via a WYSIWYG interface and allows users to alter the HTML code to fine tune website elements.

Inbound link: A link that directs an Internet user to a website from a separate website. Inbound links are used by search engines as a factor to determine where a web page ranks in search listings compared to all other websites containing the same keywords used by a search engine user.

Internet Service Provider (ISP): A company that provides Internet service for individual or business users. ISPs often offer dial up and high speed Internet connection packages based on an individual user's preferences, location, and budget. When a user connects to the Internet, the ISP logs a series of numbers (called an IP address) which helps trace illegal or unethical activity to a particular computer.

JPEG or JPG files: An image file type that is compatible with most Internet browsers. Only static images are compatible with the JPEG format. Animated images should be saved as GIF files or multimedia file types, such as Flash or AVI.

Keyword: A word or phrase that a website owner believes search engine users will use when conducting a search query. When a search engine user types in a search query, the search engine finds all websites containing the keywords and lists them for the user. Website owners load their site content with keywords to try to gain higher prominence in the listings returned to the user.

Keyword density: The percentage of words in a section of website text that is comprised of keywords. Keyword density is one of the factors a search engine uses to decide where a web page ranks in relation to all other websites that contain the same keywords. Most Internet marketers believe the optimal keyword density for a web page is between 1 and 4 percent, and many marketers design web content with a keyword density of at least 2 percent.

Link: A section of text in a web page that is coded to direct a visitor to another page on the same website, or a page on a different website, when the visitor clicks on the text. Links are coded in HTML in the format <a href="http.www.sitename.com">Click Here</a>, for example.

Memory card: A hardware component of a personal computer that allows the computer to process software applications, operating system processes, and other common computer functions. The power of a memory card is expressed as megabytes or gigabytes of RAM. The greater the RAM, the quicker a computer can process tasks and the greater the number of tasks the computer can handle at once.

Merchant account: A special bank account used to process credit card transactions on your website. Merchant account providers typically charge setup and monthly maintenance fees for credit card acceptance and authorization services and charge a percentage of each transaction that is processed through the merchant account.

Meta tag: A short block of text used to describe the contents of a web page to a search engine spider. An Internet marketer may write meta tags that are comprised entirely of keywords in an effort to boost a page's search engine ranking for specific keywords.

MP3: An audio file type that is commonly used to upload music and other audio to the Internet and transfer it among users. MP3 files can also easily be downloaded to iPhones and other portable media devices, making them ideal for creating portable music libraries. Musicians often place MP3 files on websites and allow visitors to download these files for a fee.

Opt in: A website visitor's acknowledgement that he or she has voluntarily subscribed to an email marketing list by giving the website owner his or her contact information. Opt in is also used to refer to double opt in, a process by which a subscriber clicks a link in an email to verify that he or she wishes to be included in the website owner's email marketing list.

Outbound link: A link that directs a website visitor to a different website. Outbound links may be used to provide information to a visitor that is not available on the website containing the link. Internet marketers may also place outbound links to affiliate sites to gain revenue.

Page title: A short block of text used to describe a web page. In Internet Explorer browsers, the text appears in the blue bar at the top of the page. Internet marketers load page titles with keywords in an effort to boost a web page's ranking in search engine listings for specific keywords.

PayPal: A website that allows online businesspeople to accept payments without a subscription to a merchant account. PayPal deducts a percentage of payments made via their website and deposits the remainder into an account that sellers can withdraw from. Withdrawals from PayPal accounts can be made directly to personal or business checking accounts or via checks mailed to the sellers.

Podcast: A podcast is a digital audio (MP3) presentation that one can create and add to websites, such as blogs.

Processor: Computer hardware that is the gateway for all a computer's functions. Processors with higher power ratings assist a computer with handling tasks more quickly and processing more tasks at once.

Random Access Memory (RAM): Memory on a personal computer that is used to handle software and operating system processes. RAM is expressed in megabytes or gigabytes. The greater the amount of RAM, the more smoothly a computer can execute multiple processes.

Search directory: A compilation of web page listings divided into multiple categories to facilitate ease of use. Websites submitted to a search directory are reviewed and categorized by human editors, rather than search engine spiders. As a result, search directory users typically find more relevant results in directory listings than in search engine listings.

Search engine: A website that allows users to enter keywords to find websites with content relevant to their search. Search engines use programs called spiders to read, evaluate, and index web pages for inclusion into the search engine's database.

Search engine optimization (SEO): A process of refining content on a web page, blog, or article to include keywords in the optimal density and placement for high rankings in search engines. SEO also utilizes link building to improve rankings for a web page or website.

Site map: A web page or document that contains a complete listing of all website pages and subpages. Site maps can be useful for visitors who are unfamiliar with navigating a complex website. Site maps also help website owners ensure all pages on a website are being reviewed and indexed by search engine spiders.

Social marketing: Social marketing refers to marketing that is designed to promote the common good of a community or group rather than to promote a product or service.

Social Media: Social media includes websites and applications that allow users to create and share content or to participate in social networking.

Software: Programs that are designed to allow a computer to perform certain functions. Examples of software include games, website creation tools, finance applications, and word processing programs.

Sound card: Computer hardware that allows audio files to be played on a computer's built in or external speakers. Higher quality sound cards reproduce audio that is closer to true stereo sound than stock sound cards included with commonly available computer system packages. A high-quality sound card is essential for musicians who sell their songs or compilations via the Internet.

Spam: An unsolicited email message sent by a person or business to solicit sales, transmit viruses and other malware, or carry out other questionable activity. Transmission of spam violates United States federal law, and prolific use of spam can result in fines and imprisonment of the sender.

Spider: A software application used by search engines to review and index web pages for inclusion in its search engine listings. Spiders can read web page text and links but cannot read images. Search engine spiders regularly scour the Internet for new content; however, a website owner can submit his site to search engines to have his or her site reviewed and indexed by search engine spiders more quickly.

Terms of Use: The rules decided upon by the owner or administrator of a website or discussion board regarding how users may and may not add information to the site or use the information contained within the site. Users who violate the terms of use may have their content removed from the site and may be banned from the site for intentional or repeated violations.

Traffic: The number of visitors that access a web page during a specified period. The higher the traffic received by a web page, the more popular it is and the more useful it is for generating sales and email marketing subscriptions.

Universal Resource Locator (URL): A designated name that allows web browsers to find a specific web page via the Internet. Each page of a website is assigned a specific URL that cannot be used by any other web page, whether part of the same website or a different website.

Video card: Computer hardware that allows images on a computer or on the Internet to be displayed on the computer's monitor. High quality video cards produce higher resolution, greater image clarity, and smoother animation than stock video cards included with commonly available computer system packages. A high-quality video card is essential for graphic artists and other visual artists that sell their creative works on the Internet.

Web host: A provider that allows a website owner to store website files on its server and allows users to access those files from that server. Web hosts may also offer other services to assist website owners in publishing a fully functional website, such as CGI bins, website templates, or site creation software.

Web page: A part of a website that has a specific URL that is unique to that page. Web pages may be used to separate website content that is used for different purposes, such as art gallery pages, contact pages, and FAQ pages.

Website: A dedicated collection of pages on the Internet that are linked to each other and are used to promote a business, make products and services available to Internet users, or provide information. Individual pages that comprise a website are assigned specific URLs that uniquely identify the pages and allow users to find the pages via an Internet browser, search engine, or search directory.

Website creation software: A software application that allows a user to design and create his or her own website without the assistance of a professional web designer or programmer. Some website creation software packages, such as those commonly offered by website hosting providers, offer templates a website owner can customize to create his or her website. Other website creation software utilizes a WYSIWYG interface that allows users to drag and drop elements to provide a greater level of customization. Software that uses a WYSIWYG interface often provides access to a website's HTML code, so users can fine tune the design and content of their web pages.

Wi-Fi: Wireless Internet access, which is accessed by a wireless card included with many phones and computers. Wi-Fi may be accessed from a signal provided by a wireless router connected to a desktop computer or from a satellite transmission hosted by a large ISP. Many restaurants and coffee shops in the United States now offer free Wi-Fi access to patrons as a means of attracting and retaining customers.

WYSIWYG: An acronym for What You See Is What You Get. Popular website creation software titles offer users a WYSIWYG interface to facilitate the creation of web pages without knowledge of HTML or other website coding languages. Through a WYSIWYG interface, users can drag and drop elements such as text, graphics, and video into a web page markup, and the software will automatically generate the HTML code necessary to display the web page on an Internet browser.

Shipping Your Works

After you have packaged an item you have sold online, you will need to arrange the shipment. There are a few things you should consider when choosing how to ship your item:

- *The shipping costs.* Although you will usually be able to pass your shipping costs on to your customers, you will want to keep these costs as low as possible. Your customers will not want to pay more in shipping costs than for the artwork itself, so it may not be feasible to use a shipping service to package and ship your artworks. In general, the lower the shipping costs for an item, the more customers will be willing to pay for your works. If a client buys more than one work, you may also want to combine shipping for the items by packaging them in the same box.

- *The shipping time.* Customers who purchase your works through your website or eBay auctions (learn about eBay in Chapter 9) will be very excited about receiving their artwork. Deciding how you will package and ship a particular item before you place it online for sale will help you reduce the time between when the customer purchases your item and when he or she receives it.

- *Where your customer is located.* Large packages may be difficult to ship internationally, and they may take two weeks or more to reach your customers. If an international client purchases one of your works, you may want to let him or her know up front that it may take a while for their package to arrive. If your client is used to purchasing items internationally, he or she will usually understand and will not be deterred from completing the purchase.

- *How to pack.* When it comes to knowing how to pack, you must first consider what you are packing and where it is going. Obviously, if you are sending something fragile, you need to be extra careful. Every item has its own packing requirements. Here is a helpful link about packing artwork of various types: http://reddotblog.com/how-to-ship-paintings-a-step-by-step -guide-for-artists-and-galleries.

- *The weight and size of the package.* Commercial shipping services such as UPS, DHL, FedEx, and USPS have restrictions on the weight and size of packages that can be shipped. For example, packages shipped via UPS must be under 150 pounds and must have a combined length and girth of less than 165 inches.

To determine whether your package meets this size requirement, you must determine the length and girth of your package. The length is the measurement of the longest side of your package. The girth is the total measurement of the height and width of your package multiplied by two.

For example, suppose you are shipping a package that is 60 inches by 40 inches by 6 inches. The length of your package is 60 inches, and the girth is 90 (or 46 x 2). The total measurement of the package, therefore, is 152 inches, which is under the maximum shipping size allowed by UPS.

You may want to offer free shipping on artwork that sells for more than a certain amount during period when sales are slow. Keeping shipping costs low will allow you to offer this promotion more economically, so you can still make a substantial profit from your sales. You might also try to find a local packing and shipping company that can do the job for you. However, this service will cut into your profits.

You can purchase packaging supplies at your local shipper, or order them from major shipping companies like **www.usps.com**, **www.ups.com**, **www .fedex.com**, or **www.dhl.com**. Ordering your packaging supplies online will save you the time that you would have otherwise spent driving to your local shipping store to pick up supplies.

You can save even more money by buying your shipping supplies at **www .uline.com**. Uline carries a wide variety of cardboard boxes in many different sizes, as well as bubble wrap, plastic wrap, packaging tape, and any other supplies you may need to package your works securely. If a customer receives a damaged item, you will be expected to compensate the customer, which will cut into your profits even more. Either way, it's good in include a packing slip that states who the item is for, what the item is, where it is going, and where it came from, along with your contact information. You can download a packing slip template at: **https://help.xero.com/us /Q_PackingSlip.**

Bibliography

"10 Things You May Not Know About Etsy." *Zacks Investment Research.* N.p., 29 Apr. 2015. Web.

Borchardt, Debra. "Watch Out Michael's: Etsy Is Entering The $44 Billion Craft Supplies Marketplace." *Forbes.* N.p., 15 Feb. 2017. Web.

Cain, Abigail, and Isaac Kaplan. "5 Things You Need to Know about the Booming Online Art Market." *Artsy.* N.p., 21 Apr. 2016. Web.

"From Shoe Sales to Weird Collectables: 12 Amazing Facts about EBay." *BT.com.* N.p., 7 Sept. 2015. Web. 2017.

Read, Robert. "Hiscox Online Art Trade Report 2017." *Hiscox UK.* N.p., 2016. Web.

Weinswig, Deborah. "Art Market Cooling, But Online Sales Booming." *Forbes.* Forbes Magazine, 13 May 2016. Web.

Index

A

Adobe Dreamweaver CC 11, 52, 151, 187

Artfire 9, 96, 97, 99, 104-106, 118, 187

ArtPal 112, 187

Artplode 113, 187

Artsy 10, 109, 121, 123, 135, 185, 187

Auction 10, 24, 75, 121, 124-135, 147, 170, 187

Autoresponders 11, 142, 153, 154, 171, 187

AWeber 155, 187

B

Blog 7, 24, 26, 39, 43, 48, 49, 69-71, 73, 74, 83, 85, 95, 97, 98, 103, 105, 106, 115, 125, 134, 140, 142, 145, 156, 171, 178, 187

Blogring 71, 187

Bot shop 89, 187

Brand 6, 26, 29, 39, 101, 171, 187

C

CafePress 116, 187

CGI 11, 52, 54, 152-154, 170, 172, 179, 187

Craigslist 116-118, 144, 187

D

Discussion Board 23, 24, 91-95, 172, 179, 187

Domain 6, 22, 46-48, 173, 187

E

Ebay 9, 10, 25, 41, 64, 92, 93, 96, 109, 121, 123-127, 129-135, 170, 181, 185, 187

Email 2, 10, 19, 22, 49, 51, 52, 55, 86, 89, 102, 105-108, 113,

115, 127, 137-145, 152-155, 170-173, 176, 178, 179, 187

Etsy 9, 39, 97, 99-104, 106, 108, 111, 118, 124, 134, 185, 187

F

Facebook 8, 26, 83, 85-89, 97, 108, 112, 113, 124, 163, 187

Financial 6, 11, 29, 43, 44, 147, 148, 157-159, 172, 174, 187

Fine Art America 113, 163, 187

Flickr 8, 87, 88, 187

Foap 114, 187

FormBreeze 154, 155, 187

G

Gallery 18, 20, 21, 23, 24, 41, 42, 49, 54, 57, 70, 79, 97, 98, 112, 113, 124, 126, 134, 135, 140, 141, 163, 173, 179, 187

GetResponse 155, 187

H

Handmade at Amazon 9, 97, 99, 106, 107, 111, 187

I

Imagekind 113, 114, 187

Instagram 8, 86-88, 108, 187

Instant Messenger 89, 187

iTunes 114, 187

L

LinkedIn 8, 90, 187

Listing 54, 66, 80, 103, 108, 113, 124, 128-134, 147, 170, 178, 187

M

Marketing 7, 8, 18-26, 36, 41, 42, 69, 76, 79-85, 90, 93, 95, 96, 98, 102, 107, 113, 124-126, 137-139, 143, 152-155, 157, 159, 162, 169, 170, 173, 176, 178, 179, 187

N

Newsletter 52, 102, 103, 142, 173, 187

O

OfferUp 117, 118, 187

OneStatFree 11, 156, 187

P

PageBreeze 11, 152, 154, 187

Patreon 116, 187

Payment 9, 10, 80, 102, 105, 107, 116, 118, 147-151, 187

Pinterest 8, 25, 88, 97, 99, 108, 142, 187

Podcast 115, 139, 177, 187

S

Search Engine 7, 22, 23, 59, 61-67, 69-71, 74-76, 82, 131, 145, 169, 175-180, 188

Snapchat 8, 88, 188

Social Media 8, 82-88, 97, 103, 105, 108, 112, 113, 115, 137, 138, 142, 178, 188

Software 10, 11, 14, 22, 27, 30-32, 34, 35, 43, 44, 48, 51, 52, 58, 66, 89, 106, 115, 118, 145, 147, 148, 151, 152, 155, 157, 158, 160, 170, 174, 176-180, 188

Spreesy 9, 96, 97, 99, 108, 109, 111, 188

StatCounter 11, 155, 156, 188

T

Twitter 8, 19, 83, 86, 87, 97, 99, 103, 105, 108, 112, 113, 188

V

VarageSale 117, 188

Y

YouTube 26, 49, 115, 139, 162, 163, 188